Blue Economy Strategies: Advancing Marine Policy, Ocean Governance, Sustainable Fisheries, Renewable Energy, Biodiversity, and Coastal Management

I0023014

Copyright

Blue Economy Strategies: Advancing Marine Policy, Ocean Governance, Sustainable Fisheries, Renewable Energy, Biodiversity, and Coastal Management

© 2025 Robert C. Brears

ISBN (eBook): 978-1-991368-19-5

ISBN (Paperback): 978-1-991368-20-1

Published by Global Climate Solutions

First Edition, 2025

Cover design and interior layout by Global Climate Solutions

Table of Contents

Introduction

The Blue Economy is rapidly emerging as a central concept in global discussions on sustainable development, marine policy, and climate resilience. As the world turns increasing attention to the ocean's vast potential, the Blue Economy offers a framework that integrates economic growth, social equity, and environmental protection in the stewardship of marine and coastal resources. Its influence now extends far beyond traditional maritime sectors, reaching into areas such as renewable energy, biotechnology, carbon sequestration, and digital innovation—reshaping how societies value, use, and manage the ocean.

At its core, the Blue Economy recognizes the ocean as a source of wealth, well-being, and opportunity, but also as a finite and vulnerable system. Oceans cover more than 70 percent of the planet, support a rich diversity of life, and regulate the Earth's climate, making their health essential to human survival and prosperity. They provide food, jobs, transport, energy, recreation, and cultural value to billions of people. However, increasing human pressures—overfishing, pollution, habitat loss, and the accelerating impacts of climate change—threaten the integrity of marine ecosystems and the services they provide.

The challenge and opportunity of the Blue Economy lie in shifting from exploitative, short-term approaches to integrated, long-term management that supports both people and planet. This requires policies and investments that not only drive economic development, but also conserve biodiversity, restore degraded habitats, reduce emissions, and build resilience to shocks. It means engaging all stakeholders, from coastal communities and Indigenous Peoples to global businesses and international organizations, in designing solutions that are fair, inclusive, and adaptive.

Marine policy plays a pivotal role in shaping the Blue Economy. International agreements, national legislation, and regional cooperation form the governance architecture for balancing access, rights, and responsibilities in the ocean. Science-based management, monitoring, and enforcement are vital to ensure sustainable use and equitable benefit-sharing, while innovative financial mechanisms unlock the capital needed for infrastructure, technology, and conservation. The integration of digital tools, data systems, and participatory processes is transforming how decisions are made and how marine spaces are managed.

This book provides a comprehensive exploration of the Blue Economy and marine policy, examining their principles, drivers, governance structures, sectoral opportunities, and future directions. Each chapter addresses a critical dimension of ocean management, from sustainable fisheries and aquaculture to marine renewable energy, transport, pollution control, and investment frameworks. The aim is to provide a practical and forward-looking guide for policymakers, professionals, researchers, and all those with a stake in the ocean's future.

By understanding the interconnected challenges and opportunities of the Blue Economy, and by adopting integrated, evidence-based approaches to marine policy, societies can secure a healthier, more equitable, and prosperous ocean for generations to come.

Chapter 1: Foundations of the Blue Economy

Chapter 1 lays the groundwork for understanding the Blue Economy by exploring its core concepts, historical development, and guiding principles. The Blue Economy represents a significant shift in how society views and manages ocean resources, moving from traditional, extractive uses toward an integrated approach that balances economic growth with social and environmental objectives. This chapter traces the evolution of marine resource use, examines the foundational principles of sustainability in marine systems, and highlights the importance of valuing marine resources and ecosystem services. It also discusses the major drivers and global trends influencing the Blue Economy, as well as its interconnections with the United Nations Sustainable Development Goals. By establishing a clear conceptual and policy context, this chapter provides the essential background needed to understand subsequent discussions on governance, sectoral opportunities, and emerging challenges within the Blue Economy.

Defining the Blue Economy

The Blue Economy is a holistic framework that seeks to promote economic growth, improved livelihoods, and social equity while ensuring the sustainable use of ocean, sea, and coastal resources. Unlike traditional ocean-based industries that often prioritize short-term gains over environmental protection, the Blue Economy places sustainability, stewardship, and inclusivity at its core. It recognizes that healthy marine ecosystems are fundamental to long-term economic prosperity and human well-being, and that responsible governance of these natural assets is critical for both current and future generations.

At its essence, the Blue Economy extends beyond conventional sectors like fisheries, shipping, and oil and gas extraction, to embrace a diverse range of ocean-related activities. These include renewable energy generation from offshore wind, wave, and tidal sources; sustainable aquaculture and mariculture; biotechnology and marine genetic resources; ecotourism and recreation; and the conservation and restoration of critical habitats such as coral reefs, mangroves, and seagrass beds. By adopting an integrated and inclusive approach, the Blue Economy fosters innovation and encourages the development of new markets that can create jobs, drive investment, and contribute to food and energy security, all while safeguarding the ecological integrity of marine and coastal environments.

A key distinction of the Blue Economy is its commitment to valuing both the tangible and intangible benefits provided by the ocean. This includes not only the direct economic value of goods and services but also the broader ecosystem services that underpin climate regulation, carbon sequestration, nutrient cycling, and coastal protection. By internalizing these values into policy and investment decisions, the Blue Economy supports a shift toward circular, restorative, and resilient economic models that are compatible with planetary boundaries.

The Blue Economy is also characterized by an emphasis on equity and inclusivity. It seeks to ensure that the benefits of marine resource use are shared fairly among all stakeholders, including local communities, Indigenous Peoples, and Small Island Developing States (SIDS), whose cultures, identities, and economies are closely tied to the ocean. Participatory governance, capacity building, and access to education, technology, and finance are seen as essential elements for achieving a truly inclusive Blue Economy that leaves no one behind.

Historical Evolution of Marine Resource Use

Throughout history, human societies have depended on the oceans for food, transportation, and trade. The earliest records of marine resource use date back thousands of years, with coastal communities harvesting shellfish, fish, and seaweed using traditional methods closely attuned to local ecosystems. These early practices were

8

largely small-scale and sustainable, shaped by an intimate understanding of seasonal cycles and the regenerative capacity of marine environments.

With the advent of advanced navigation and shipbuilding technologies, maritime exploration expanded during the Age of Discovery from the 15th to the 17th centuries. Oceans became vital highways for global trade, connecting continents and enabling the movement of people, goods, and ideas on an unprecedented scale. This period saw the emergence of large-scale commercial fishing and the exploitation of new marine resources, including whales for oil and baleen, as well as cod and herring for expanding European markets. While these activities contributed to economic development, they also marked the beginning of intensified pressures on ocean ecosystems.

The Industrial Revolution in the 18th and 19th centuries further transformed marine resource use. Steam-powered vessels enabled longer voyages and greater cargo capacities, increasing the reach and intensity of fishing fleets and facilitating the global exchange of marine products. Technological advances in fishing gear, refrigeration, and preservation methods allowed for greater harvests, but also accelerated the depletion of key species and the degradation of coastal habitats. This era saw the rise of industrial whaling and the development of commercial ports, leading to significant changes in coastal landscapes and the structure of marine industries.

The 20th century brought both new opportunities and challenges. The discovery and extraction of offshore oil and gas reserves opened a new frontier in marine resource use, bringing economic growth but also raising environmental risks. Advances in marine science led to a better understanding of the complexity and interconnectedness of ocean systems, and evidence of overfishing, pollution, and habitat destruction prompted the first calls for conservation and management. International treaties and agreements, such as the United Nations Convention on the Law of the Sea (UNCLOS), began to formalize marine governance, setting the stage for modern marine policy.

Today, the historical evolution of marine resource use reflects a transition from subsistence and local-scale activities to global industries with far-reaching impacts. This legacy underscores the need for an integrated, sustainable approach to managing the world's oceans, balancing economic, social, and ecological priorities within the framework of the Blue Economy.

Principles of Sustainability in Marine Systems

Sustainability in marine systems centers on ensuring that ocean resources are managed and used in ways that maintain ecological integrity, support economic vitality, and foster social well-being for present and future generations. The principles of sustainability in this context are designed to guide decision-makers, industries, and communities toward practices that protect and enhance the resilience of marine ecosystems while enabling the continued provision of goods and services.

A core principle is the maintenance of ecosystem health. This means safeguarding the diversity, productivity, and natural functions of marine habitats, species, and ecological processes. Protecting keystone species, preserving critical habitats like coral reefs, mangroves, and seagrass meadows, and preventing the loss of biodiversity are essential to maintaining the balance and productivity of ocean systems. Sustainable management requires recognizing and respecting ecological limits, ensuring that human activities do not exceed the regenerative capacity of marine environments.

Another key principle is the adoption of a precautionary approach. Given the complexity of marine systems and the uncertainties associated with environmental change, policy and management should err on the side of caution when scientific knowledge is incomplete or when the potential for irreversible harm exists. This approach is especially important in fisheries management, pollution control, and the introduction of new technologies, ensuring that actions taken today do not compromise the ocean's health in the long term.

Integrated management is also fundamental to marine sustainability. Oceans are dynamic and interconnected, influenced by natural processes and human activities across multiple sectors and jurisdictions. Effective stewardship requires coordination among stakeholders, integration of policies across sectors such as fisheries, energy, tourism, and shipping, and a holistic understanding of land-sea interactions. Marine spatial planning (MSP), ecosystem-based management, and collaborative governance frameworks are tools that support integration and coherence in policy and practice.

Equity and inclusivity form another pillar of sustainable marine systems. Sustainability means ensuring that benefits are shared fairly among current stakeholders and future generations, with particular attention to the rights and roles of coastal communities, Indigenous Peoples, and vulnerable groups. Access to resources, capacity building, and participation in decision-making are essential for social acceptance and the durability of sustainability initiatives.

Finally, sustainability in marine systems requires adaptive management. This involves monitoring outcomes, learning from experience, and being responsive to new information, technological advances, and changing environmental conditions. An adaptive approach helps build resilience, allowing marine systems and the societies that depend on them to thrive amid uncertainty and change.

Economic Valuation of Marine Resources

The economic valuation of marine resources is a fundamental component of the Blue Economy, as it provides a systematic approach for recognizing, quantifying, and integrating the full range of benefits derived from the ocean into policy, management, and investment decisions. Traditionally, the economic value of marine resources was primarily measured through the direct market returns of industries such as fisheries, shipping, oil and gas extraction, and coastal tourism. However, this approach often overlooked the broader array of ecosystem services and non-market benefits provided by healthy oceans.

Modern economic valuation frameworks seek to capture the true wealth of marine resources by accounting for both market and non-market values. Market values are relatively straightforward to measure and include the income generated from harvesting seafood, mineral extraction, maritime transport, and recreational activities. Non-market values, on the other hand, reflect the vital ecosystem services oceans provide—such as carbon sequestration, coastal protection, nutrient cycling, climate regulation, and support for biodiversity—which underpin the long-term productivity and resilience of marine environments.

Methods for valuing these non-market benefits include cost-benefit analysis, contingent valuation, ecosystem service modeling, and natural capital accounting. These approaches help decision-makers weigh the economic, social, and environmental trade-offs associated with different uses of marine resources. For example, maintaining healthy mangrove forests may provide greater long-term economic value through coastal protection, carbon storage, and fisheries support than short-term conversion for development.

Incorporating economic valuation into marine policy has several important implications. First, it highlights the hidden costs of ecosystem degradation and the benefits of conservation, making a compelling case for investing in the protection and sustainable management of ocean resources. Second, it enables the design of economic instruments—such as taxes, subsidies, and payment for ecosystem services—that can align incentives with sustainability goals. Third, it helps ensure that marine resource use decisions reflect not just private gains but also public goods and long-term societal interests.

Economic valuation also plays a key role in promoting social equity. By recognizing and assigning value to the benefits that coastal communities and Indigenous Peoples derive from marine resources, policies can be better tailored to protect traditional livelihoods and support inclusive economic growth. Ultimately, comprehensive valuation frameworks support a shift toward sustainable, ecosystem-based management by providing a clearer picture of the full economic significance of the world's oceans.

Ecosystem Services and Natural Capital

Ecosystem services are the benefits that humans derive from healthy marine and coastal ecosystems, forming the foundation of natural capital—the world's stock of natural assets that include geology, soil, air, water, and all living organisms. In the context of the Blue Economy, understanding and preserving these services is essential for ensuring the long-term sustainability and productivity of ocean resources.

Marine ecosystems deliver a diverse range of ecosystem services, often categorized into four main groups: provisioning, regulating, supporting, and cultural services. Provisioning services refer to tangible products obtained from the ocean, such as fish, shellfish, seaweed, and salt, which contribute directly to food security, nutrition, and economic livelihoods. Regulating services are those that help control environmental conditions, including climate regulation through carbon sequestration by mangroves, seagrasses, and phytoplankton, as well as coastal protection from storms and erosion provided by coral reefs and wetlands.

Supporting services underpin the functioning of marine ecosystems themselves. These include nutrient cycling, primary production, and the maintenance of genetic diversity, which are fundamental to the resilience and health of the entire marine environment. Cultural services reflect the non-material benefits people gain from the sea, encompassing recreation, tourism, spiritual values, and cultural identity—especially significant for many coastal and island communities.

Natural capital represents the economic value embedded in these ecosystem services. The concept encourages policymakers and stakeholders to recognize marine ecosystems as valuable assets that yield both direct and indirect benefits to society. This approach shifts perspectives from viewing the ocean as an inexhaustible resource to seeing it as a form of capital that requires investment, stewardship, and careful management to maintain its value over time.

Preserving ecosystem services and natural capital is central to the Blue Economy because degradation of marine environments—through pollution, overfishing, habitat destruction, or climate change—leads to the loss of these critical benefits. Assessing and accounting for ecosystem services in decision-making enables more informed trade-offs between economic development and environmental protection. By integrating the value of natural capital into policies, marine planning, and financial systems, societies can prioritize actions that maintain or enhance ecosystem functions, ensuring the health, resilience, and prosperity of both the ocean and the communities that depend on it.

Drivers and Trends in the Global Blue Economy

The global Blue Economy is shaped by a complex interplay of drivers and emerging trends that influence how marine resources are used, managed, and governed. These forces reflect both longstanding and new opportunities and challenges, as societies seek to balance economic growth with the need for environmental sustainability and social equity.

One of the principal drivers of the Blue Economy is the growing recognition of the ocean's critical role in supporting livelihoods and national economies. Coastal and island nations increasingly see the sustainable use of marine resources as essential for food security, job creation, poverty reduction, and economic diversification. This is particularly evident in sectors such as fisheries, aquaculture, tourism, and renewable energy, where expanding demand and investment are spurring innovation and infrastructure development.

Technological advancement is another key driver, enabling new possibilities for ocean observation, monitoring, and exploitation. Advances in satellite imaging, remote sensing, and data analytics improve the understanding of marine systems and support more effective management. Meanwhile, innovations in marine biotechnology, ocean energy, and digitalization are opening new frontiers for economic activity, including sustainable aquaculture, marine genetic resource utilization, and smart shipping.

Environmental and climate concerns are reshaping priorities within the Blue Economy. The impacts of climate change—such as sea-level rise, ocean acidification, and extreme weather events—underscore the need for adaptive and resilient marine policy. At the same time, there is growing awareness of the importance of restoring ocean health by reducing pollution, protecting biodiversity, and adopting ecosystem-based management practices. International agreements and policy frameworks, such as the United Nations Sustainable Development Goals and global climate accords, are increasingly guiding national strategies and investments.

A significant trend is the rise of public-private partnerships and innovative financing models. Blue bonds, impact investment, and payment for ecosystem services mechanisms are being adopted to mobilize capital for sustainable ocean initiatives. These financial tools help bridge gaps between conservation goals and economic imperatives, fostering cross-sectoral collaboration and enabling the scaling of sustainable solutions.

Finally, social and governance trends are playing a vital role. There is growing emphasis on inclusive governance, stakeholder participation, and the recognition of the rights and knowledge of Indigenous Peoples and local communities. Transparent, equitable, and science-based decision-making processes are now seen as prerequisites for long-term success in the Blue Economy.

Together, these drivers and trends are transforming the way the world views and interacts with the ocean, steering marine policy toward a more integrated, innovative, and sustainable future.

Interlinkages with Sustainable Development Goals

The Blue Economy is inherently connected to the United Nations Sustainable Development Goals (SDGs), reflecting the critical role of healthy oceans in advancing global sustainability, prosperity, and equity. Among the 17 SDGs, Goal 14—Life Below Water— explicitly focuses on the conservation and sustainable use of oceans, seas, and marine resources. However, the Blue Economy supports and is supported by many other SDGs through its emphasis on integrated resource management, social inclusion, and environmental stewardship.

For instance, sustainable fisheries and aquaculture contribute to Goal 2 (Zero Hunger) by enhancing food security and nutrition, while job creation in coastal industries addresses Goal 8 (Decent Work and Economic Growth). The development of renewable ocean energy, such as offshore wind and tidal power, advances Goal 7 (Affordable and Clean Energy) and helps mitigate climate change under Goal 13 (Climate Action). Protection and restoration of marine and coastal ecosystems are central to Goal 15 (Life on Land), as many land-based livelihoods depend on the health of adjacent marine environments.

The Blue Economy's focus on inclusive governance and equitable benefit sharing is closely tied to Goal 10 (Reduced Inequalities) and Goal 16 (Peace, Justice and Strong Institutions), recognizing the importance of empowering marginalized groups, local communities, and Small Island Developing States. Furthermore, international collaboration and partnerships in ocean research, technology transfer, and financing support Goal 17 (Partnerships for the Goals).

By embedding marine sustainability within broader development objectives, the Blue Economy reinforces the interconnected nature of the SDGs. Progress in one area—such as improved ocean health— can drive advances across multiple goals, creating synergies that strengthen resilience, foster innovation, and promote long-term well-being for people and planet alike.

Chapter 2: Global Governance and International Marine Policy

Chapter 2 explores the global frameworks and international policy instruments that underpin the governance of the world's oceans. As the ocean spans national borders and supports a vast array of interconnected economic, environmental, and social interests, effective international cooperation is essential for sustainable management. This chapter examines the evolution and architecture of global marine governance, beginning with the UNCLOS and extending to regional frameworks, key international organizations, and binding agreements. It addresses the challenges and complexities of ocean governance, including issues of equity, access, and the special roles of Small Island Developing States and coastal nations. By clarifying the roles, responsibilities, and mechanisms for collaboration among countries and organizations, this chapter sets the stage for understanding how global policy shapes national action, supports sustainable development, and responds to emerging challenges in the Blue Economy.

Overview of International Law of the Sea

International law of the sea forms the legal foundation for the governance, use, and protection of the world's oceans and seas. Its framework defines the rights and responsibilities of states and other actors in relation to maritime zones, resource exploitation, environmental protection, and navigational freedoms. The evolution of international law of the sea has been shaped by centuries of maritime activity, increasing demand for marine resources, and the need to balance competing interests among nations.

The modern law of the sea is anchored in the UNCLOS, adopted in 1982 and often described as the "constitution for the oceans." UNCLOS provides a comprehensive legal framework that delineates maritime zones, including internal waters, territorial seas, contiguous zones, exclusive economic zones (EEZs), continental shelves, and the high seas. Each zone is associated with specific rights and duties.

For example, coastal states exercise sovereignty in their territorial sea up to 12 nautical miles from the baseline, while the EEZ extends 200 nautical miles, granting rights over natural resources but also obligating states to protect and preserve the marine environment.

Freedom of navigation is a cornerstone of international law of the sea, allowing ships of all states—regardless of flag—to move freely on the high seas and in EEZs, subject to certain restrictions and responsibilities. UNCLOS also addresses critical issues such as the conservation of marine living resources, the prevention of marine pollution, and the conduct of marine scientific research.

Dispute resolution is another important aspect of the international law of the sea. UNCLOS establishes mechanisms for the peaceful settlement of disputes, including the International Tribunal for the Law of the Sea (ITLOS), arbitration, and the International Court of Justice (ICJ). These mechanisms help maintain order and address conflicts over maritime boundaries, resource rights, and environmental obligations.

The international law of the sea continues to evolve as new challenges emerge, such as the management of BBNJ, the regulation of new marine activities, and the response to climate change impacts. Its principles and provisions are central to shaping effective, fair, and sustainable marine policy on a global scale, underpinning the cooperation and stewardship required for the Blue Economy.

UNCLOS

The UNCLOS is the principal international treaty governing the use and conservation of the world's oceans and seas. Adopted in 1982 and entering into force in 1994, UNCLOS provides a legal framework that addresses almost every aspect of ocean space, from navigation and resource rights to environmental protection and dispute resolution. Today, UNCLOS has been ratified by over 165 parties, making it a near-universal foundation for marine governance.

One of the landmark achievements of UNCLOS is its establishment of clearly defined maritime zones. These include the territorial sea (up to 12 nautical miles from the baseline), contiguous zone (up to 24 nautical miles), EEZ, (up to 200 nautical miles), and the continental shelf, where coastal states have special rights to explore and exploit natural resources. Beyond national jurisdiction lie the high seas, which remain open to all states and are subject to international rules that protect freedoms such as navigation, overflight, and the laying of submarine cables and pipelines.

UNCLOS codifies a balance between the rights of coastal states and the interests of the international community. It recognizes the sovereignty of states over their territorial waters, while requiring them to allow innocent passage for foreign vessels. In the EEZ, coastal states enjoy exclusive rights to exploit and manage living and non-living resources, but are also obligated to conserve the marine environment and cooperate with other states on matters such as migratory fish stocks and marine pollution.

Environmental stewardship is a core principle of UNCLOS. The Convention requires parties to protect and preserve the marine environment, prevent and control pollution, and conduct environmental impact assessments for activities that may cause harm. It also provides the legal basis for marine scientific research, ensuring that research activities are conducted peacefully and for the benefit of all.

UNCLOS is underpinned by robust mechanisms for the peaceful settlement of disputes, including the International Tribunal for the Law of the Sea, arbitration panels, and the International Court of Justice. These institutions help resolve conflicts over boundaries, resource rights, and compliance with treaty obligations.

Overall, UNCLOS is a cornerstone of modern marine policy, facilitating cooperation, promoting sustainable resource use, and supporting the development of the Blue Economy in an increasingly interconnected world.

Regional Marine Policy Frameworks

Regional marine policy frameworks play a crucial role in bridging global principles with local action, enabling countries that share seas or coastal areas to collaboratively manage and protect their marine resources. These frameworks recognize that many ocean challenges—such as overfishing, pollution, and habitat loss—are transboundary by nature, requiring coordinated solutions that reflect regional ecological, economic, and cultural contexts.

Regional frameworks are typically established through intergovernmental agreements, conventions, or organizations. Examples include the Regional Seas Programmes under the United Nations Environment Programme (UNEP), the European Union's Marine Strategy Framework Directive, the Caribbean Community fisheries agreements, and the Helsinki Convention for the Protection of the Marine Environment of the Baltic Sea. These instruments set common standards and objectives for marine protection, pollution control, and sustainable resource management among participating states.

One of the main functions of regional marine frameworks is to harmonize policies and regulations across national boundaries. This approach helps address the movement of pollutants, the migration of marine species, and shared resource stocks, ensuring that actions taken in one country support broader regional objectives. Joint monitoring, data sharing, and coordinated enforcement are core elements that underpin the effectiveness of these frameworks.

Regional frameworks also facilitate capacity building, technical assistance, and the exchange of best practices among member states. By pooling resources and expertise, countries can respond more effectively to emerging threats and opportunities, such as climate change adaptation, the restoration of critical habitats, and the development of sustainable fisheries and aquaculture. In many cases, regional organizations provide platforms for stakeholder engagement, bringing together governments, industry, scientists, and civil society to collaboratively design and implement solutions.

Another important aspect is the ability of regional frameworks to support the implementation of international commitments, such as the UNCLOS and the SDGs. By translating these global agreements into practical regional strategies, countries are better positioned to achieve both national and collective goals for marine sustainability.

In a rapidly changing world, regional marine policy frameworks offer flexible and adaptive mechanisms for managing shared seas, fostering cooperation, and advancing the Blue Economy. Their role is increasingly vital as nations confront complex marine challenges that cannot be addressed by individual states alone.

International Organizations and Agreements

International organizations and agreements are central to the governance of the world's oceans, providing the structure, coordination, and guidance necessary to address global marine challenges and advance the objectives of the Blue Economy. Through these mechanisms, states collaborate to ensure the sustainable use, conservation, and equitable sharing of marine resources across jurisdictional boundaries.

The United Nations (UN) is the leading forum for international cooperation on ocean issues, primarily through agencies such as the United Nations Division for Ocean Affairs and the Law of the Sea and the United Nations Environment Programme (UNEP). UNEP administers the Regional Seas Programme, which brings together neighboring countries to protect shared marine environments. The Intergovernmental Oceanographic Commission of UNESCO facilitates global cooperation in ocean science, research, and capacity building, advancing knowledge and the sustainable management of marine systems.

Other key organizations include the International Maritime Organization (IMO), which sets global standards for shipping safety, security, and marine environmental protection, and the Food and Agriculture Organization (FAO), which leads efforts in fisheries and aquaculture governance through the Code of Conduct for Responsible Fisheries and related instruments. The International Seabed Authority regulates the exploration and exploitation of mineral resources in areas beyond national jurisdiction, ensuring that activities are conducted for the benefit of humanity as a whole while minimizing environmental impacts.

Global agreements complement the work of these organizations, providing legal frameworks and commitments for marine policy. Besides the UNCLOS, significant agreements include the Convention on Biological Diversity (CBD), the International Convention for the Prevention of Pollution from Ships (MARPOL), and regional fisheries management agreements. These treaties set out rules and obligations for the conservation of marine biodiversity, prevention of marine pollution, and sustainable use of ocean resources.

International organizations and agreements also play a critical role in fostering dialogue, knowledge sharing, and technical cooperation. They enable states to address issues that transcend national borders, such as illegal, unreported, and unregulated (IUU) fishing, climate change impacts, and the protection of vulnerable marine ecosystems. Through regular meetings, assessments, and reporting mechanisms, these bodies facilitate accountability, transparency, and the progressive development of marine policy at the global scale.

As ocean challenges grow more complex, the role of international organizations and agreements will continue to expand, supporting the evolution of marine governance and the sustainable growth of the Blue Economy.

Ocean Governance Challenges

Governing the world's oceans presents a unique set of challenges due to the vastness, complexity, and interconnectedness of marine environments. Unlike terrestrial systems, oceans span national boundaries and include areas beyond the jurisdiction of any single state, making cooperation and coordinated management essential. The multifaceted nature of ocean governance means that addressing environmental, economic, and social objectives often involves balancing competing interests, managing uncertainty, and overcoming significant institutional and enforcement barriers.

One major challenge is the fragmentation of governance frameworks. Multiple international, regional, and national bodies have overlapping responsibilities for marine resource management, environmental protection, and maritime security. This fragmentation can lead to gaps, duplication of efforts, conflicting mandates, and inefficient use of resources. For example, regional fisheries management organizations (RFMOs), environmental conventions, and sectoral agencies may operate independently, making it difficult to implement truly integrated and ecosystem-based approaches to ocean management.

Another pressing challenge is the lack of adequate data, monitoring, and enforcement capabilities. The sheer scale of the ocean, coupled with limited technological and financial resources in many countries, hampers the ability to detect illegal activities, monitor ecosystem health, and enforce regulations. This is particularly acute in areas beyond national jurisdiction, such as the high seas, where the absence of clear ownership and authority complicates efforts to address overfishing, pollution, and biodiversity loss.

Equity and access also present significant governance concerns. The benefits and burdens of ocean use are not distributed evenly, with coastal communities, Indigenous Peoples, and Small Island Developing States (SIDS) often facing barriers to participation and influence in decision-making processes. Ensuring that governance structures are inclusive, transparent, and accountable is critical for promoting fair and equitable outcomes and for building legitimacy and support for marine policy.

Emerging threats—such as climate change, ocean acidification, and the proliferation of new marine activities like deep-sea mining—add further complexity. These issues require adaptive governance mechanisms capable of responding to uncertainty, integrating new scientific knowledge, and anticipating future risks.

Addressing ocean governance challenges demands stronger international cooperation, the integration of policies across sectors and scales, investment in monitoring and enforcement, and a commitment to equity and participation. As ocean use intensifies, effective governance is essential for safeguarding marine ecosystems, supporting the Blue Economy, and securing benefits for current and future generations.

Equity and Access in Marine Policy

Equity and access are fundamental principles in marine policy, ensuring that the benefits and opportunities arising from ocean resources are shared fairly and that all stakeholders have a meaningful voice in decision-making. Historically, marine resource management and policy have often favored powerful actors or industrial interests, overlooking the rights, needs, and knowledge of coastal communities, Indigenous Peoples, and Small Island Developing States (SIDS). Addressing these imbalances is critical for achieving truly sustainable and inclusive outcomes in the Blue Economy.

Equity in marine policy involves recognizing and rectifying disparities in how marine resources are allocated, used, and governed. This means safeguarding the rights of marginalized groups to access fisheries, coastal lands, and marine spaces that are central to their livelihoods, food security, and cultural heritage. It also requires acknowledging traditional knowledge systems and customary practices, which have sustained marine ecosystems for generations and can inform more effective, locally adapted policy solutions.

Access goes beyond physical availability of resources to include participation in governance and decision-making. Inclusive marine policy frameworks provide mechanisms for stakeholder engagement, ensuring that local communities, women, youth, and other underrepresented groups can influence the development and implementation of policies that affect their lives. Transparent, participatory processes build trust, strengthen social cohesion, and improve compliance with regulations, leading to more durable and effective management outcomes.

The principle of equity extends to the fair distribution of economic benefits generated by the Blue Economy. Mechanisms such as benefit-sharing agreements, community quotas, and capacity-building initiatives help ensure that profits from fisheries, tourism, renewable energy, and other sectors reach those who depend most on healthy oceans. Equitable access to education, technology, and financial resources further empowers communities to participate in new opportunities and adapt to changing conditions.

Marine policy must also address intergenerational equity, considering the rights of future generations to enjoy healthy and productive oceans. This long-term perspective encourages the adoption of precautionary and ecosystem-based management approaches that avoid irreversible harm and promote the resilience of marine environments.

Embedding equity and access at the heart of marine policy supports social justice, reduces conflict, and fosters the legitimacy necessary for successful marine governance. As the Blue Economy expands, prioritizing these principles is vital for building inclusive, resilient, and sustainable marine societies.

The Role of Small Island Developing States and Coastal Nations

Small Island Developing States (SIDS) and coastal nations play a pivotal role in the stewardship and advancement of the Blue

Economy. Despite their relatively small land areas and limited economic resources, these countries possess vast ocean territories, rich biodiversity, and deep cultural connections to marine environments. Their unique vulnerabilities to climate change, sea-level rise, and ocean degradation underscore the urgency of developing and implementing sustainable marine policies.

SIDS and coastal nations are often at the forefront of innovation in marine management and policy. They have pioneered approaches such as ecosystem-based fisheries management, community-led conservation, and the establishment of large marine protected areas. These efforts are driven not only by the need to sustain local livelihoods and food security, but also by a deep commitment to preserving ocean health for future generations. Many SIDS advocate for stronger international action on issues like climate adaptation, ocean pollution, and the protection of BBNJ, raising the global profile of these critical challenges.

Access to international support and capacity building is essential for these countries to fully participate in and benefit from the Blue Economy. Partnerships with international organizations, donor agencies, and research institutions help address gaps in financing, technology, and expertise. At the same time, SIDS and coastal nations bring valuable knowledge, leadership, and perspectives to global forums, ensuring that the needs and priorities of vulnerable communities are reflected in international marine policy.

The experiences and leadership of SIDS and coastal nations highlight the importance of inclusive governance, equitable benefit-sharing, and integrated approaches to ocean management. As the world seeks to expand the Blue Economy, these countries serve as both custodians of marine biodiversity and champions for sustainable, resilient ocean futures.

Chapter 3: Marine Spatial Planning and Integrated Coastal Zone Management

Chapter 3 examines the critical role of MSP and integrated coastal zone management (ICZM) in achieving balanced, sustainable use of ocean and coastal resources. As human activities in marine and coastal areas become increasingly diverse and intensive, competition for space and resources grows, creating the need for coordinated, science-based approaches to planning and management. This chapter introduces the fundamentals of MSP and ICZM, highlighting their principles, processes, and legal foundations. It explores how these tools align economic development, conservation, and social objectives, while addressing stakeholder interests and reducing conflicts. By focusing on practical implementation, stakeholder engagement, technological advancements, and adaptive management, this chapter demonstrates how integrated planning frameworks are essential for building resilient coastal communities, safeguarding marine ecosystems, and supporting the long-term success of the Blue Economy.

Fundamentals of Marine Spatial Planning

MSP is a strategic, science-based process for analyzing and allocating the spatial and temporal distribution of human activities in marine environments. Its primary objective is to balance ecological, economic, and social goals by organizing the use of ocean space in a way that reduces conflicts, supports sustainable development, and conserves marine ecosystems. As human activities in the ocean—such as shipping, fisheries, aquaculture, tourism, renewable energy, and conservation—continue to grow, MSP has emerged as an essential tool for integrated ocean governance.

At its core, MSP involves bringing together multiple stakeholders, including governments, industry, scientists, local communities, and non-governmental organizations, to develop comprehensive plans for how marine areas are to be used and managed. This collaborative approach ensures that diverse interests are considered, trade-offs are addressed, and synergies are maximized, resulting in more informed and broadly supported decisions.

The MSP process begins with the collection and analysis of spatial data on the physical, biological, and socio-economic characteristics of marine and coastal areas. This information forms the basis for mapping current uses, identifying sensitive habitats and ecological hotspots, and assessing potential areas for development or protection. Effective MSP relies on robust scientific knowledge, advanced geospatial technologies, and participatory methods to ensure the best available information guides decision-making.

A defining feature of MSP is its focus on ecosystem-based management, which recognizes the interconnectedness of species, habitats, and human activities. This approach seeks to maintain ecosystem health and services while accommodating sustainable use. MSP also addresses cumulative impacts, considering how different activities interact and affect marine environments over time.

MSP is designed to be adaptive and iterative, allowing for regular review and revision of plans as new information emerges or conditions change. Clear objectives, transparent processes, and effective monitoring and evaluation are essential components for successful implementation.

Ultimately, marine spatial planning helps align diverse interests, reduce user conflicts, and enhance the long-term sustainability of marine resources. By providing a framework for coordinated decision-making, MSP supports the balanced development of the Blue Economy while safeguarding the health and resilience of ocean ecosystems.

Principles of Integrated Coastal Zone Management

ICZM is a holistic approach designed to promote the coordinated and sustainable management of coastal zones, where land, sea, and human activities intersect. Recognizing the complex and dynamic nature of coastal environments, ICZM brings together multiple stakeholders, sectors, and levels of government to harmonize policies, reduce conflicts, and address cumulative impacts. The goal is to support both ecological integrity and socioeconomic development, ensuring that coastal resources remain productive and resilient for current and future generations.

A central principle of ICZM is integration—across sectors, spatial scales, and time. This means aligning policies and planning efforts in areas such as fisheries, tourism, urban development, transportation, conservation, and disaster risk reduction. Integration also involves linking actions taken on land with their effects in the sea, recognizing that many coastal challenges—such as pollution, habitat loss, and erosion—are driven by land-based activities and watershed dynamics.

ICZM is guided by the precautionary and ecosystem-based approaches. The precautionary approach encourages managers to act conservatively in the face of scientific uncertainty, while the ecosystem-based approach ensures that management decisions maintain ecological processes, biodiversity, and natural productivity. Together, these approaches help prevent irreversible environmental damage and support long-term coastal health.

Stakeholder participation is fundamental to ICZM. Meaningful engagement of local communities, Indigenous Peoples, industry, scientists, and non-governmental organizations strengthens decision-making, builds local ownership, and increases compliance with management measures. Inclusive processes help identify trade-offs, foster consensus, and ensure that a diversity of knowledge and values are incorporated into planning and policy.

Adaptive management is another core principle. Coastal systems are dynamic and subject to natural variability, climate change, and socioeconomic shifts. ICZM frameworks are designed to be flexible, allowing for monitoring, learning, and adjustment of strategies in response to changing conditions and new information.

Equity and sustainability underpin all aspects of ICZM. Ensuring fair access to resources, protecting the rights of vulnerable groups, and balancing short-term gains with long-term well-being are essential for the legitimacy and durability of management efforts.

By embedding these principles, ICZM supports the sustainable use, conservation, and resilience of coastal zones, aligning human activities with the natural dynamics of the coast and fostering the integration needed for effective Blue Economy development.

Legal and Institutional Arrangements

Legal and institutional arrangements are the backbone of effective marine spatial planning and integrated coastal zone management, providing the framework through which policies are developed, implemented, and enforced. These arrangements define the rights, responsibilities, and authorities of various stakeholders and set the rules for how marine and coastal resources are accessed, used, and protected.

At the national level, countries typically establish laws and regulations that delineate jurisdictional boundaries, authorize planning processes, and identify lead agencies responsible for marine and coastal governance. These frameworks may include legislation specific to environmental protection, fisheries, shipping, energy development, and land-use planning, as well as cross-sectoral laws that enable integrated management. Clear legal mandates are essential for coordinating action across different government departments and for preventing conflicts among competing uses.

Institutional arrangements involve the establishment of dedicated agencies, inter-ministerial committees, or multi-stakeholder platforms tasked with developing and implementing marine spatial plans and coastal management strategies. These bodies often operate at multiple levels—national, regional, and local—ensuring that policies are aligned and adapted to the specific ecological and socioeconomic context of each area. Effective institutions facilitate communication, data sharing, and stakeholder engagement, creating the conditions necessary for inclusive and adaptive governance.

Regional cooperation is also critical, especially in transboundary marine areas where resources and impacts are shared. Countries may enter into regional agreements or participate in organizations that coordinate policies, set standards, and support joint monitoring and enforcement. Examples include regional fisheries management organizations, marine environmental conventions, and the regional seas programs. These institutions help harmonize legal frameworks and foster collaboration among neighboring states.

International law, particularly the UNCLOS, provides an overarching legal context for marine and coastal governance. UNCLOS establishes the rights and duties of states in maritime zones and sets obligations for the protection and sustainable use of marine resources. Other global agreements, such as the Convention on Biological Diversity and the IMO's conventions, further shape national and regional legal frameworks.

Robust legal and institutional arrangements are essential for translating policy objectives into concrete action, ensuring accountability, and adapting management approaches in response to new challenges. By providing clarity, consistency, and coordination, these arrangements enable the sustainable development and protection of marine and coastal environments within the Blue Economy.

Stakeholder Engagement and Participatory Approaches

Stakeholder engagement and participatory approaches are central to the success of MSP and ICZM. By actively involving all relevant actors—governments, industry, local communities, Indigenous Peoples, scientists, and non-governmental organizations—these processes ensure that diverse perspectives, needs, and knowledge systems inform the development and implementation of marine and coastal policies. Meaningful engagement enhances the legitimacy, effectiveness, and sustainability of management outcomes.

A key principle of stakeholder engagement is inclusivity. Effective participatory processes identify and reach out to all groups affected by or interested in marine resource use, especially those who have historically been marginalized or underrepresented, such as small-scale fishers, women, and Indigenous communities. Early and ongoing engagement helps build trust, reduce conflicts, and foster ownership of decisions, making it more likely that policies will be respected and followed in practice.

Participatory approaches take many forms, including public consultations, community meetings, workshops, advisory committees, and collaborative management arrangements. These methods create opportunities for stakeholders to share their knowledge, express their concerns, and contribute ideas for solutions. In some cases, co-management agreements give communities a formal role in resource governance, recognizing their traditional knowledge and granting them a stake in decision-making.

Transparency is another fundamental aspect of stakeholder engagement. Clear communication about objectives, processes, and anticipated outcomes ensures that stakeholders understand how their input will be used and what influence they have over final decisions. Providing accessible information and feedback mechanisms enables stakeholders to make informed contributions and hold decision-makers accountable.

Engagement must also be tailored to local contexts, acknowledging cultural norms, language barriers, and varying levels of technical expertise. Building capacity through education, training, and access to relevant information empowers stakeholders to participate effectively and meaningfully.

The benefits of participatory approaches extend beyond improved policy outcomes. Involving stakeholders fosters social learning, strengthens community resilience, and encourages stewardship of marine and coastal resources. When people feel heard and valued, they are more likely to support and contribute to sustainable management initiatives.

Incorporating stakeholder engagement and participatory approaches as standard practice in MSP and ICZM ensures that marine governance is not only technically sound but also socially just, adaptive, and resilient—qualities that are essential for advancing the Blue Economy.

Tools and Technologies for Marine Planning

The advancement of tools and technologies has transformed the practice of MSP and ICZM, making it possible to gather, analyze, and visualize complex data that support informed decision-making. These technologies enable planners, policymakers, and stakeholders to better understand marine environments, assess potential impacts, and design more effective management strategies for sustainable use of ocean and coastal resources.

Geographic Information Systems (GIS) are among the most widely used tools in marine planning. GIS allows for the integration and spatial analysis of diverse datasets—such as bathymetry, habitat distribution, human activities, and ecosystem services—into detailed, interactive maps. These visualizations make it easier to identify spatial conflicts, ecological hotspots, and suitable zones for various uses, from conservation to development.

Remote sensing technologies, including satellite imagery and aerial drones, provide high-resolution, real-time data on oceanographic conditions, land use, water quality, and changes in coastal habitats. These tools enhance monitoring and surveillance capabilities, enabling rapid detection of illegal activities, pollution events, or ecosystem changes that may require intervention.

Oceanographic sensors and autonomous monitoring platforms, such as underwater gliders and buoys, continuously collect information on physical, chemical, and biological parameters. Data from these systems help track changes in temperature, salinity, currents, and biological productivity, offering insights into ecosystem health and resilience.

Decision support systems (DSS) combine scientific data, stakeholder input, and scenario modeling to evaluate management options and predict outcomes. DSS platforms enable planners to explore trade-offs between different uses, optimize spatial allocation, and assess the long-term impacts of policy choices under varying environmental or economic conditions.

Emerging digital tools—such as artificial intelligence, machine learning, and big data analytics—are increasingly being applied to marine planning. These technologies can process vast amounts of information, identify patterns, and generate recommendations that enhance adaptive management and responsiveness to change.

Publicly accessible web portals and mobile applications further facilitate stakeholder engagement by making data, plans, and monitoring results available to a broad audience. These tools support transparency, education, and collaborative decision-making.

By leveraging advanced tools and technologies, marine planners can develop integrated, adaptive, and science-based solutions that are essential for achieving the goals of the Blue Economy while safeguarding marine and coastal ecosystems.

Addressing Conflicts and Trade-offs

MSP and ICZM inevitably involve managing conflicts and trade-offs among a wide array of users, interests, and ecosystem needs. The increasing intensity and diversity of ocean and coastal activities—such as fishing, shipping, tourism, renewable energy, conservation, and mineral extraction—often lead to competing demands for the same space and resources. Effectively addressing these conflicts is essential for achieving balanced, sustainable outcomes in the Blue Economy.

The first step in managing conflicts is the early identification and mapping of existing and potential uses, users, and areas of ecological significance. Spatial analysis tools, participatory mapping, and stakeholder consultations are used to pinpoint overlaps, hotspots, and areas of tension. Transparent sharing of this information with all parties creates a shared understanding of the challenges and opportunities, building a foundation for constructive dialogue.

Stakeholder engagement is central to resolving conflicts. Inclusive, participatory processes bring together representatives from different sectors, local communities, and other interest groups to discuss priorities, voice concerns, and negotiate solutions. Facilitated workshops, mediation, and consensus-building exercises can help clarify values, identify common ground, and develop acceptable compromises. Recognizing and respecting traditional rights, cultural values, and local knowledge are especially important when addressing conflicts involving Indigenous Peoples and small-scale resource users.

Trade-off analysis is a key tool for evaluating the economic, social, and environmental consequences of alternative management scenarios. Decision support systems can model the outcomes of different options, making explicit the benefits and costs associated with each. This helps decision-makers weigh short-term gains against long-term sustainability, balance sectoral objectives, and minimize negative impacts on vulnerable ecosystems and communities.

Adaptive management approaches ensure that conflicts and trade-offs are not seen as one-time decisions, but as part of an ongoing, flexible process. Regular monitoring, feedback, and periodic revision of plans allow for adjustments as new information emerges, conditions change, or unintended impacts arise.

Addressing conflicts and trade-offs in MSP and ICZM supports more equitable, efficient, and durable solutions. By fostering cooperation, transparency, and shared responsibility, these processes build trust and resilience, enabling marine and coastal systems to deliver benefits for both people and nature within the Blue Economy framework.

Monitoring, Evaluation, and Adaptive Management

Monitoring, evaluation, and adaptive management are essential components of successful MSP and ICZM. These processes provide the feedback needed to assess whether objectives are being met, to detect changes in environmental and social conditions, and to guide continuous improvement in management strategies.

Monitoring involves the systematic collection of data on key ecological, social, and economic indicators. This may include tracking the health of marine habitats, water quality, biodiversity, resource use, compliance with regulations, and stakeholder satisfaction. Robust monitoring systems help identify trends, emerging threats, and the effectiveness of interventions, providing the evidence needed for informed decision-making.

Evaluation builds on monitoring by analyzing results against established goals and benchmarks. It assesses whether management measures are achieving their intended outcomes, identifies successes and shortcomings, and reveals areas for adjustment. Evaluation processes often involve regular reporting, independent reviews, and the participation of stakeholders to ensure transparency and accountability.

Adaptive management is a dynamic approach that incorporates monitoring and evaluation findings into ongoing decision-making. Rather than relying on fixed plans, adaptive management recognizes the uncertainty and complexity of marine systems. It emphasizes learning by doing, experimenting with new approaches, and making changes as new information becomes available or as conditions evolve. This approach enables managers to respond effectively to unexpected challenges, emerging opportunities, and advances in scientific understanding.

By integrating monitoring, evaluation, and adaptive management into MSP and ICZM, practitioners can ensure that marine and coastal management remains responsive, resilient, and capable of delivering sustainable outcomes over time. This continuous learning process strengthens the ability to achieve long-term objectives in the face of environmental variability, socioeconomic change, and new policy priorities.

Chapter 4: Sustainable Fisheries and Aquaculture

Chapter 4 delves into the essential role of sustainable fisheries and aquaculture within the Blue Economy, highlighting their contributions to food security, livelihoods, and economic growth worldwide. As global demand for seafood rises and marine ecosystems face mounting pressures, the need for responsible management and innovation in these sectors has never been greater. This chapter provides an overview of the state of global fisheries and aquaculture, exploring the challenges of overexploitation, environmental impacts, and social equity. It discusses policy approaches and management frameworks for achieving sustainability, including ecosystem-based fisheries management, the establishment of marine protected areas, and the adoption of certification schemes. Additionally, the chapter examines technological innovations and market mechanisms that support responsible practices, while addressing persistent threats such as illegal, unreported, and unregulated fishing. By drawing connections between ecological health, economic opportunity, and governance, this chapter offers guidance for advancing sustainable fisheries and aquaculture as vital pillars of the Blue Economy.

Overview of Global Fisheries and Aquaculture

Fisheries and aquaculture are vital components of the global Blue Economy, providing food security, livelihoods, and economic value for millions of people around the world. These sectors supply a significant portion of the world's animal protein, support coastal and rural economies, and play an important role in cultural traditions and community identities. However, they also face a complex set of challenges related to sustainability, resource management, and environmental impacts.

Capture fisheries, which involve the harvesting of wild fish and other marine species, have long been a cornerstone of food systems and trade. Global fish production has grown steadily over the past decades, but many wild fish stocks are now fully exploited or overexploited, placing increasing pressure on marine ecosystems. Overfishing, bycatch, IUU fishing, and habitat destruction threaten the long-term viability of capture fisheries and the well-being of communities that depend on them. Ensuring the sustainability of wild fisheries requires robust management measures, science-based catch limits, effective enforcement, and international cooperation.

Aquaculture—the farming of fish, shellfish, seaweed, and other aquatic organisms—has expanded rapidly to meet growing demand and to compensate for the stagnation or decline of wild fisheries. Today, aquaculture accounts for more than half of global seafood production. This sector presents opportunities for economic diversification, rural development, and technological innovation. However, aquaculture is not without challenges. Environmental concerns include water pollution, disease outbreaks, the escape of farmed species, and the conversion of critical habitats such as mangroves for fish ponds. Social issues, such as equitable access to resources and the rights of small-scale producers, also require attention.

Both fisheries and aquaculture are shaped by national policies, international agreements, and market forces. Certification schemes, traceability initiatives, and sustainability standards are increasingly used to improve practices and provide assurances to consumers. The adoption of ecosystem-based management, precautionary approaches, and stakeholder participation is gaining traction as a way to balance production, conservation, and social goals.

Advances in technology, monitoring, and data collection are helping to address some of the challenges faced by these sectors, while climate change introduces new uncertainties and risks. Going forward, the resilience and sustainability of global fisheries and aquaculture will depend on adaptive management, responsible practices, and inclusive policies that recognize the interconnectedness of ocean health, food security, and human development.

Policy Approaches for Sustainable Fisheries

Sustainable fisheries management is critical for preserving marine biodiversity, supporting livelihoods, and ensuring the long-term availability of seafood. Policy approaches for sustainable fisheries aim to balance ecological health with economic and social needs, addressing both local and global challenges through a combination of regulatory, economic, and participatory tools.

Central to sustainable fisheries policy is the implementation of science-based catch limits and harvest controls. Setting quotas or total allowable catches based on robust stock assessments helps prevent overfishing and allows depleted populations to recover. These measures are supported by monitoring, control, and surveillance systems that track catches, enforce compliance, and deter IUU fishing activities.

Rights-based management approaches, such as individual transferable quotas (ITQs) or community-based access rights, allocate secure shares of the resource to fishers or fishing communities. These systems provide incentives for responsible stewardship and can reduce the "race to fish," promoting more stable and profitable fisheries over time. Territorial Use Rights in Fisheries and co-management arrangements, where local communities share decision-making authority with government agencies, have proven effective in fostering compliance and sustainable practices.

Marine protected areas (MPAs) and spatial management tools are increasingly integrated into fisheries policy. By restricting or regulating fishing in designated zones, MPAs can help conserve essential habitats, protect spawning grounds, and build resilience against environmental shocks. Zoning plans, seasonal closures, and gear restrictions further support the recovery of vulnerable species and habitats.

Market-based instruments, such as eco-labeling and certification schemes, create incentives for fisheries to adopt sustainable practices and provide consumers with the option to choose responsibly sourced seafood. These programs often require compliance with strict environmental and social standards, increasing transparency and traceability in seafood supply chains.

Participatory approaches are also fundamental to sustainable fisheries policy. Engaging fishers, Indigenous Peoples, scientists, and other stakeholders in the design and implementation of management measures builds trust, incorporates diverse knowledge, and improves the legitimacy and effectiveness of policies.

Adapting to emerging challenges—such as climate change, ocean acidification, and shifting fish distributions—requires flexible, adaptive management frameworks. Continuous monitoring, research, and the ability to adjust policies in response to new information ensure that fisheries remain productive and resilient in a changing world.

Ecosystem-Based Fisheries Management

Ecosystem-Based Fisheries Management (EBFM) is an integrated approach that seeks to manage fisheries within the broader context of marine ecosystems, recognizing the complex interdependencies among species, habitats, and human activities. Unlike traditional management, which often focuses on individual species or stocks in isolation, EBFM emphasizes the health and functioning of the entire ecosystem, aiming to maintain ecological balance, biodiversity, and resilience while supporting sustainable fisheries.

A key principle of EBFM is the consideration of ecosystem structure and processes in decision-making. This includes understanding food webs, predator-prey relationships, habitat requirements, and the impacts of fishing on non-target species and ecosystem functions. By accounting for these interactions, EBFM aims to prevent unintended consequences, such as the collapse of dependent species or the degradation of critical habitats.

In practice, EBFM incorporates a range of management tools and strategies. Spatial measures, such as MPAs, no-take zones, and habitat restoration projects, help safeguard essential breeding and nursery grounds. Effort controls, gear restrictions, and bycatch reduction measures are used to minimize impacts on vulnerable species and habitats. EBFM also advocates for the protection of ecosystem services—such as nutrient cycling, water purification, and carbon sequestration—that underpin both fisheries productivity and broader environmental health.

Adaptive management is central to EBFM, reflecting the inherent uncertainty and variability of marine systems. Regular monitoring of ecological indicators, environmental conditions, and fishing activities allows for timely adjustments to management measures as new information emerges or conditions change. This flexible, learning-oriented approach increases the resilience of both ecosystems and fisheries in the face of climate change and other stressors.

Stakeholder participation is essential for effective EBFM. Engaging fishers, scientists, Indigenous communities, and other stakeholders ensures that diverse knowledge systems and values are integrated into management decisions. Collaborative governance builds trust, facilitates compliance, and supports the successful implementation of ecosystem-based approaches.

Ecosystem-Based Fisheries Management offers a pathway toward more sustainable, productive, and resilient fisheries. By moving beyond single-species management to embrace the complexity of marine ecosystems, EBFM contributes to the conservation of biodiversity, the maintenance of ecosystem services, and the long-term viability of the Blue Economy.

Marine Protected Areas and Conservation Tools

MPAs and other conservation tools are vital strategies for safeguarding ocean biodiversity, supporting fisheries sustainability, and enhancing the resilience of marine ecosystems. MPAs are defined geographic areas where human activities are regulated or restricted to achieve specific conservation objectives, such as preserving habitats, protecting endangered species, and maintaining ecological processes. The design and implementation of MPAs are guided by scientific evidence and often involve stakeholder input to ensure effectiveness and social acceptance.

MPAs range in type and level of protection, from fully protected no-take reserves, where all extractive activities are prohibited, to multiple-use areas that allow limited and regulated resource use. No-take zones are particularly effective in restoring depleted fish populations, conserving critical habitats, and providing spillover benefits to adjacent fisheries. By protecting spawning and nursery grounds, MPAs help maintain the productivity and health of both target and non-target species.

Beyond MPAs, a range of conservation tools can complement traditional management approaches. Temporal closures restrict fishing or other activities during critical periods, such as breeding seasons, to enhance the recovery of vulnerable species. Gear restrictions, such as bans on destructive fishing practices like bottom trawling or the use of certain types of nets, reduce habitat damage and bycatch of non-target organisms. Habitat restoration projects, including coral reef rehabilitation and mangrove replanting, help rebuild essential ecosystem functions and services.

Effective implementation of MPAs and conservation tools requires strong legal and institutional frameworks, clear objectives, adequate enforcement, and ongoing monitoring and evaluation. Transparent processes and active stakeholder engagement are essential for building support, addressing potential conflicts, and ensuring that local communities benefit from conservation outcomes.

Adaptive management is also key. Marine environments are dynamic, and conservation measures must be responsive to new scientific information, changing ecological conditions, and shifting social and economic contexts. Regular assessment of the effectiveness of MPAs and other tools allows for adjustments and improvements over time.

By combining spatial protection, regulatory measures, restoration efforts, and adaptive management, MPAs and conservation tools contribute significantly to the conservation of marine biodiversity and the sustainable use of ocean resources. These approaches play a crucial role in supporting the goals of the Blue Economy and ensuring the long-term health of marine ecosystems for future generations.

Innovations in Sustainable Aquaculture

Sustainable aquaculture is evolving rapidly, driven by the need to meet rising global demand for seafood while minimizing environmental impacts and supporting the health of aquatic ecosystems. Innovations in this sector are transforming traditional practices, introducing new technologies, and developing alternative approaches that address challenges related to resource use, pollution, disease, and ecosystem resilience.

One major area of innovation is the adoption of integrated multi-trophic aquaculture (IMTA) systems. IMTA involves cultivating different species—such as fish, shellfish, and seaweeds—together in a way that mimics natural ecosystem relationships. In these systems, the byproducts (e.g., waste) from one species serve as nutrients for others, reducing environmental impacts, improving resource efficiency, and diversifying production. IMTA helps close nutrient loops, enhance water quality, and increase the overall productivity and profitability of aquaculture operations.

Recirculating aquaculture systems (RAS) represent another significant advancement. RAS are land-based, closed-loop systems that continuously filter and reuse water, dramatically reducing water consumption and the risk of pollution or escape of farmed species into natural environments. These systems offer better control over growing conditions, reduce disease outbreaks, and enable aquaculture to be sited away from sensitive coastal habitats.

Innovations in feed development are also shaping the future of sustainable aquaculture. Traditionally, aquaculture feeds have relied heavily on wild-caught fishmeal and fish oil, contributing to pressure on marine resources. Today, researchers and companies are developing alternative feeds using plant proteins, insect meal, algae, and microbial sources. These alternatives can significantly lower the environmental footprint of aquaculture and improve the sector's overall sustainability.

Selective breeding and biotechnology are contributing to disease resistance, faster growth rates, and better adaptation to varying environmental conditions. Advances in monitoring technologies—such as real-time water quality sensors, remote cameras, and automated feeding systems—are enhancing farm management, reducing waste, and improving animal health.

Regulatory frameworks and certification schemes, such as the Aquaculture Stewardship Council (ASC), are encouraging the adoption of best practices and transparent standards. These initiatives incentivize producers to minimize impacts on habitats, ensure responsible sourcing, and protect the welfare of workers and local communities.

The combination of technological innovation, ecological design, and responsible management is enabling aquaculture to become a more sustainable and resilient contributor to food security and economic development, aligning with the principles of the Blue Economy.

Market Mechanisms and Certification Schemes

Market mechanisms and certification schemes are powerful tools for promoting sustainability and responsible practices in global fisheries and aquaculture. By creating incentives for producers to improve environmental and social performance and providing consumers with trustworthy information, these approaches help shift markets toward products that support the long-term health of marine ecosystems and the well-being of communities.

One of the most prominent market mechanisms is eco-labeling, where seafood products that meet specific sustainability criteria are marked with a recognizable label. The Marine Stewardship Council and the ASC are two leading organizations that certify wild-caught and farmed seafood, respectively. Products bearing these labels must adhere to rigorous standards related to stock management, ecosystem impacts, traceability, and social responsibility. Eco-labeling helps consumers identify and choose seafood that is harvested or farmed in ways that minimize environmental harm and support fair labor practices.

Certification schemes go hand in hand with traceability systems, which track seafood from its source to the final point of sale. Robust traceability helps prevent IUU fishing from entering supply chains and assures buyers of product origin and compliance with sustainability standards. These systems are increasingly supported by digital technologies such as barcoding, blockchain, and electronic monitoring, which improve transparency and reduce fraud.

Market-based instruments such as fisheries improvement projects and aquaculture improvement projects bring together producers, buyers, NGOs, and other stakeholders to address specific sustainability challenges within supply chains. These collaborative efforts set clear goals, monitor progress, and encourage the adoption of better management practices through technical support and market rewards.

Financial incentives—including price premiums for certified products, preferential access to certain markets, and investment in sustainable production—further drive change. Retailers, food service companies, and institutional buyers increasingly demand proof of sustainability, amplifying the influence of market mechanisms throughout the industry.

While market mechanisms and certification schemes have proven effective in raising standards and driving improvements, challenges remain in ensuring accessibility for small-scale producers, maintaining credibility, and addressing evolving issues such as social responsibility and climate resilience. Continued innovation, stakeholder engagement, and harmonization of standards are needed to ensure these tools maximize their impact.

By harnessing market forces, certification schemes and market mechanisms play a crucial role in aligning economic incentives with sustainability, supporting the transition to more responsible and resilient fisheries and aquaculture in the Blue Economy.

Addressing Illegal, Unreported, and Unregulated Fishing

IUU fishing poses a major threat to the sustainability of marine resources, the livelihoods of legitimate fishers, and the health of ocean ecosystems. IUU fishing undermines management efforts, depletes fish stocks, damages habitats, and contributes to food insecurity and lost economic opportunities, particularly in developing coastal and island nations.

Addressing IUU fishing requires a multifaceted approach involving robust policy frameworks, effective monitoring and enforcement, and strong international cooperation. At the national level, governments can strengthen legal frameworks, enhance penalties for violations, and improve the capacity of fisheries agencies to monitor, control, and surveil fishing activities. The use of technologies such as vessel monitoring systems (VMS), electronic logbooks, and satellite-based tracking increases the ability to detect and deter illegal operations, while port state measures help prevent IUU-caught fish from entering markets.

Regional and international collaboration is essential, as IUU fishing often occurs across jurisdictional boundaries. RFMOs play a key role in coordinating enforcement, sharing intelligence, and harmonizing regulations among member states. Global agreements such as the FAO Agreement on Port State Measures and the United Nations Fish Stocks Agreement provide frameworks for collective action.

Transparency and traceability in seafood supply chains are critical for reducing the market incentives that drive IUU fishing. Certification schemes, traceability tools, and public reporting mechanisms help ensure that only legally and sustainably sourced products reach consumers. Engaging fishers, local communities, and industry stakeholders in surveillance, reporting, and compliance efforts further strengthens the fight against IUU activities.

Tackling IUU fishing is fundamental for protecting ocean biodiversity, maintaining productive fisheries, and supporting the equitable and sustainable development of the Blue Economy.

Chapter 5: Marine Biodiversity and Conservation Policy

Chapter 5 focuses on the central importance of marine biodiversity and effective conservation policy in sustaining the health, productivity, and resilience of ocean ecosystems. As human activities intensify and new pressures emerge, safeguarding marine biodiversity has become a global priority for achieving sustainable development and supporting the Blue Economy. This chapter explores the ecological significance of marine biodiversity, the array of threats facing ocean life, and the policy frameworks designed to protect vulnerable habitats and species. It discusses the role of marine protected areas, conservation tools, and the management of genetic resources both within and beyond national jurisdiction. The chapter also addresses the growing need for adaptive policy responses, international cooperation, and inclusive governance to meet emerging conservation challenges. By highlighting the interdependence of biodiversity, ecosystem services, and human well-being, this chapter underscores why marine conservation is foundational to a prosperous and resilient Blue Economy.

Significance of Marine Biodiversity

Marine biodiversity encompasses the variety of life forms found in ocean and coastal environments, from microscopic plankton to the largest whales. This rich diversity is fundamental to the health, productivity, and resilience of marine ecosystems, underpinning a vast array of ecological processes and services that benefit both nature and people.

At the most basic level, marine biodiversity sustains food webs and ecosystem functioning. Each species plays a unique role—whether as a primary producer, predator, decomposer, or habitat builder—contributing to the stability and productivity of ocean systems. Coral reefs, mangroves, seagrass meadows, and deep-sea habitats are particularly notable for their high levels of biodiversity and the essential services they provide. These ecosystems offer nursery grounds for commercially valuable fish, support nutrient cycling and carbon sequestration, and buffer coastlines against storms and erosion.

The significance of marine biodiversity extends to human well-being and economic prosperity. Healthy, diverse oceans are the foundation of sustainable fisheries and aquaculture, ensuring the availability of food and livelihoods for billions of people worldwide. Many communities—especially those in coastal and island regions—depend directly on marine biodiversity for their cultural traditions, recreation, and spiritual values.

Marine biodiversity is also a critical resource for scientific and medical discovery. Countless species harbor unique genetic material, enzymes, and chemical compounds with applications in biotechnology, pharmaceuticals, and industry. Exploring and conserving this genetic diversity opens new avenues for innovation and adaptation, particularly in a changing climate.

Importantly, biodiversity enhances the resilience of marine ecosystems. Diverse communities are better able to withstand and recover from disturbances such as disease outbreaks, pollution events, and climate-related impacts like ocean warming and acidification. The presence of multiple species with overlapping functions helps ensure that essential ecological processes continue even when conditions change.

The loss of marine biodiversity threatens the stability of ocean systems and the benefits they provide to humanity. Overfishing, habitat destruction, pollution, invasive species, and climate change are driving declines in marine life across the globe. Protecting and restoring biodiversity is therefore a cornerstone of sustainable ocean management and the Blue Economy, supporting healthy ecosystems, robust economies, and resilient societies now and in the future.

Threats to Ocean Biodiversity

Ocean biodiversity faces mounting threats from a range of human activities and environmental changes, putting at risk the health, productivity, and resilience of marine ecosystems. Understanding these threats is essential for developing effective conservation and management strategies to sustain the benefits that healthy oceans provide.

Overfishing remains one of the most significant pressures on marine biodiversity. Unsustainable harvesting depletes fish populations, disrupts food webs, and reduces genetic diversity within species. Bycatch—the unintended capture of non-target species such as sea turtles, seabirds, and marine mammals—further amplifies the impact, often resulting in the decline of vulnerable or endangered populations.

Habitat destruction and degradation pose another major threat. Coastal development, dredging, land reclamation, and destructive fishing practices such as bottom trawling can damage or eliminate critical habitats like coral reefs, mangroves, seagrass meadows, and estuaries. The loss of these habitats not only diminishes biodiversity but also weakens ecosystem functions such as nursery provision, carbon sequestration, and coastal protection.

Pollution from land-based and maritime sources continues to degrade marine environments. Nutrient runoff from agriculture leads to eutrophication and dead zones, while plastics, microplastics, oil spills, and toxic chemicals contaminate waters and harm marine life. Pollutants can accumulate in the food chain, affecting the health of entire ecosystems and the humans who depend on them.

Climate change is an increasingly urgent threat to ocean biodiversity. Rising sea temperatures cause coral bleaching, alter species distributions, and disrupt breeding and migration patterns. Ocean acidification, resulting from increased carbon dioxide absorption, impairs the ability of calcifying organisms like corals, mollusks, and some plankton to build shells and skeletons. Sea-level rise and more intense storms threaten coastal habitats and the species they support.

Invasive species introduced through ballast water, aquaculture, or shipping can outcompete native species, alter ecosystem dynamics, and reduce overall biodiversity. Disease outbreaks, sometimes exacerbated by warming waters or pollution, further threaten the balance and stability of marine communities.

The cumulative and interconnected nature of these threats amplifies their impacts, making effective management particularly challenging. Addressing the root causes of biodiversity loss—such as overexploitation, habitat alteration, pollution, and climate change—requires coordinated action at local, national, and global levels. Safeguarding ocean biodiversity is fundamental to the resilience of marine ecosystems and the sustainability of the Blue Economy.

Conservation Policy Frameworks

Conservation policy frameworks provide the legal, institutional, and strategic foundations necessary for protecting marine biodiversity and ensuring the sustainable use of ocean resources. These frameworks operate at global, regional, and national levels, setting objectives, standards, and mechanisms for conservation, restoration, and management of marine ecosystems.

At the global level, several key agreements underpin marine conservation efforts. The UNCLOS establishes broad obligations for states to protect and preserve the marine environment. The Convention on Biological Diversity (CBD) sets international targets for conserving at least 30% of coastal and marine areas by 2030 ("30 by 30"), restoring degraded ecosystems, and mainstreaming biodiversity considerations into sectoral policies. Other important agreements include the Ramsar Convention on Wetlands, the Convention on Migratory Species (CMS), and treaties addressing specific threats such as the MARPOL.

Regional policy frameworks complement global agreements by addressing the unique ecological and governance contexts of shared seas. Instruments such as the European Union's Marine Strategy Framework Directive, regional seas conventions under the United Nations Environment Programme (UNEP), and RFMOs set region-specific standards, facilitate cooperation among neighboring countries, and coordinate monitoring, enforcement, and data sharing.

National conservation frameworks translate international commitments into domestic law and action. National policies may designate MPAs, establish no-take zones, regulate fisheries, restrict pollutant discharges, and require environmental impact assessments for new developments. Integrated management plans, such as MSP and ICZM, help align conservation objectives with other ocean uses, balancing ecological integrity with economic and social needs.

A central feature of effective conservation policy is adaptive management—regularly assessing outcomes, incorporating new scientific knowledge, and adjusting measures as conditions change. Stakeholder participation, transparency, and equitable benefit-sharing are essential principles that build support for conservation actions and ensure that local communities and Indigenous Peoples are meaningfully involved.

Enforcement and compliance mechanisms—ranging from monitoring and surveillance to legal penalties—are critical for translating policy into practice. Capacity building, technology transfer, and international cooperation further strengthen the implementation of conservation frameworks.

By embedding conservation objectives within broader ocean governance, policy frameworks create the foundation for protecting biodiversity, maintaining ecosystem services, and advancing the goals of the Blue Economy in a changing world.

Protecting Vulnerable Marine Ecosystems

Vulnerable marine ecosystems—such as coral reefs, mangroves, seagrass meadows, deep-sea habitats, and polar regions—are among the most biologically diverse and ecologically significant areas of the ocean, yet they are also some of the most threatened. Protecting these ecosystems is essential for preserving biodiversity, supporting fisheries, buffering coastlines, and maintaining the broader health and productivity of the ocean.

Coral reefs, for example, are home to a quarter of all marine species and provide vital ecosystem services, including coastal protection and livelihoods for millions of people. However, they are highly sensitive to stressors such as rising sea temperatures, ocean acidification, overfishing, and pollution. Large-scale coral bleaching events and disease outbreaks have led to significant declines in reef health worldwide.

Mangroves and seagrass meadows also play critical roles. Mangroves act as natural coastal defenses, reducing the impact of storms and erosion while providing nursery habitat for fish and other marine life. Seagrass meadows contribute to water quality, store significant amounts of carbon, and support diverse communities of organisms. Both ecosystems are threatened by coastal development, land reclamation, pollution, and climate change-induced sea-level rise.

Deep-sea habitats, including cold-water coral reefs, hydrothermal vents, and seamounts, harbor unique and often poorly understood species. These environments are increasingly at risk from activities such as deep-sea fishing, mining, and the disposal of waste. The slow growth rates and limited recovery potential of many deep-sea species make these ecosystems particularly vulnerable to disturbance.

Polar regions, with their distinctive ice-dependent ecosystems, face rapid changes due to warming temperatures and the loss of sea ice. Shifts in species distributions, new shipping routes, and the potential for resource extraction add further pressure.

Protecting vulnerable marine ecosystems requires a combination of strategies: establishing and effectively managing MPAs, enforcing spatial and temporal restrictions on extractive activities, restoring degraded habitats, and addressing land-based sources of pollution. International cooperation is often necessary for transboundary or high seas ecosystems, while local stewardship and community involvement enhance protection efforts closer to shore.

Advances in monitoring, research, and adaptive management are helping identify priority areas for protection and guide conservation action. Safeguarding these ecosystems is not only vital for their intrinsic value but also for the well-being and resilience of human societies that depend on the ocean.

Marine Genetic Resources and Access

Marine genetic resources (MGRs) encompass the genetic material of marine organisms—ranging from microorganisms and algae to plants, animals, and invertebrates—that hold actual or potential value for research, innovation, and development. These resources are increasingly recognized for their vital role in biotechnology, pharmaceuticals, agriculture, food production, and industry, offering unique genetic compounds and properties that can lead to medical breakthroughs, new materials, and solutions to environmental challenges.

Access to MGRs is governed by a complex patchwork of national and international laws, reflecting both their immense value and the unique challenges associated with their collection, utilization, and benefit-sharing. Within areas under national jurisdiction, countries have sovereign rights to regulate access to MGRs, often requiring permits, benefit-sharing agreements, and compliance with biodiversity protection laws. The Convention on Biological Diversity (CBD) and its Nagoya Protocol provide an international framework for access and benefit-sharing, aiming to ensure that countries and communities providing genetic resources receive a fair share of the benefits arising from their use.

Beyond national jurisdiction, in the high seas and deep seabed, governance of MGRs has been less clear. The UNCLOS establishes the freedom of scientific research and the principle that marine resources beyond national boundaries are the common heritage of humankind. However, the lack of detailed rules on the access and equitable sharing of benefits from MGRs in these areas has led to ongoing debates and negotiations. Recent progress has been made with the adoption of the international agreement on the conservation and sustainable use of marine biological diversity of areas beyond national jurisdiction (BBNJ), which seeks to address these gaps.

Equitable access and benefit-sharing are central to the sustainable management of MGRs. Effective frameworks should recognize the interests of developing countries, Indigenous Peoples, and local communities, ensuring participation in decision-making and fair returns from research and commercialization. Transparency, capacity building, and technology transfer are also important for enabling all nations to benefit from advances in marine biotechnology.

As interest in MGRs grows, clear and fair governance is essential for promoting innovation, supporting conservation, and ensuring that the use of marine genetic resources contributes to both scientific progress and the broader goals of the Blue Economy.

Biodiversity Beyond National Jurisdiction

BBNJ refers to the vast and ecologically rich areas of the ocean that lie outside the sovereignty of any single nation—primarily the high seas and the deep seabed. These areas cover nearly two-thirds of the world's ocean and harbor a significant proportion of marine biodiversity, including unique species and habitats that are vital to global ecological processes and the health of the planet.

Historically, governance of BBNJ has been limited and fragmented. The UNCLOS provides a general legal framework for activities in the high seas, emphasizing the freedom of navigation, research, and the principle of the "common heritage of mankind" for deep-sea resources. However, it does not offer comprehensive mechanisms for conserving biodiversity or regulating emerging activities such as bioprospecting, deep-sea mining, and large-scale fishing beyond national boundaries.

The absence of clear rules and enforcement mechanisms has made BBNJ vulnerable to overexploitation, habitat destruction, and other threats. Unsustainable fishing practices, pollution, invasive species, and the impacts of climate change all contribute to the degradation of these remote and often poorly studied regions. The lack of coordinated management and monitoring further complicates conservation efforts, making it difficult to assess the status of species and ecosystems or to respond quickly to emerging risks.

Recognizing these challenges, the international community has moved to develop a new legally binding agreement under UNCLOS to address the conservation and sustainable use of BBNJ. The new agreement—often referred to as the BBNJ Treaty or "High Seas Treaty"—aims to fill governance gaps by establishing procedures for creating marine protected areas, conducting environmental impact assessments, ensuring access and benefit-sharing for marine genetic resources, and building capacity for developing countries to participate in high seas conservation.

Central to the BBNJ process is the principle of equity—ensuring that all nations, including developing countries and Small Island Developing States, have a say in decision-making and a fair share of the benefits derived from high seas biodiversity. Transparency, international cooperation, and science-based management will be crucial for effective implementation.

As human activity in areas beyond national jurisdiction continues to increase, strengthening governance and stewardship of BBNJ is essential for maintaining global ocean health, supporting resilient ecosystems, and achieving the long-term goals of the Blue Economy.

Policy Responses to Emerging Conservation Challenges

Emerging conservation challenges in the marine environment—such as climate change, ocean acidification, plastic pollution, invasive species, and the rapid expansion of offshore industries—demand adaptive and forward-looking policy responses. The dynamic and interconnected nature of these threats means that traditional, sector-specific approaches are often insufficient. Instead, effective policies are increasingly holistic, integrated, and focused on building the resilience of marine ecosystems and communities.

One key policy response is the integration of climate adaptation and mitigation into marine management. This includes protecting and restoring blue carbon habitats like mangroves, seagrass meadows, and salt marshes, which sequester significant amounts of carbon while also supporting biodiversity and coastal protection. Climate-smart marine spatial planning helps reduce vulnerabilities by factoring in projected sea-level rise, shifting species distributions, and the increased frequency of extreme events.

Addressing marine pollution—particularly plastics and emerging contaminants—requires coordinated action at local, national, and global levels. Policies include banning or restricting single-use plastics, improving waste management infrastructure, supporting circular economy approaches, and promoting innovation in materials and recycling. Enhanced monitoring and international cooperation are vital for tackling pollution that crosses borders and affects shared seas.

Managing the expansion of offshore industries and new uses of the ocean, such as renewable energy and deep-sea mining, relies on rigorous environmental impact assessments, precautionary regulation, and robust monitoring. Adaptive management frameworks allow for policies to be revised as new information and technologies emerge.

Engagement of local communities, Indigenous Peoples, and stakeholders is essential for the legitimacy and effectiveness of policy responses. Inclusive governance, transparent decision-making, and capacity-building initiatives strengthen collective action and ensure policies reflect diverse perspectives and knowledge.

By proactively addressing emerging challenges, policy frameworks can support the conservation of marine biodiversity, enhance ecosystem resilience, and secure the long-term benefits of the Blue Economy.

Chapter 6: Ocean-Based Renewable Energy and Innovation

Chapter 6 explores the dynamic field of ocean-based renewable energy and its role in driving innovation and sustainable growth within the Blue Economy. As the global demand for clean energy rises and climate change accelerates, the ocean offers vast, largely untapped potential for renewable power generation through technologies such as offshore wind, wave, tidal, ocean thermal, and salinity gradient energy. This chapter examines the main types of ocean renewable energy, the policy incentives and regulatory considerations shaping their development, and the integration of these technologies into coastal and island economies. It highlights recent advances in technology, blue carbon initiatives, and the challenges and opportunities involved in scaling up marine energy solutions. By investigating the intersection of innovation, investment, and environmental stewardship, this chapter provides a comprehensive overview of how ocean-based renewable energy can contribute to decarbonization, energy security, and the sustainable transformation of marine industries.

Types of Ocean Renewable Energy

Ocean renewable energy refers to the range of technologies and systems that harness the natural power of the sea to produce clean, sustainable energy. As nations seek alternatives to fossil fuels and aim to reduce greenhouse gas emissions, ocean energy is emerging as an important component of the global shift toward renewable resources. The diverse and largely untapped energy potential of the world's oceans offers significant opportunities for innovation, energy security, and economic development within the Blue Economy.

The most established form of ocean renewable energy is offshore wind power. Offshore wind farms use turbines mounted on fixed or floating platforms to capture wind energy over open water, where wind speeds are typically higher and more consistent than on land.

Offshore wind is rapidly expanding, particularly in Europe and Asia, and is expected to play a major role in future energy systems due to its scalability and declining costs.

Wave energy captures the kinetic and potential energy generated by surface waves as they move across the ocean. Various technologies—such as oscillating water columns, point absorbers, and attenuators—convert this movement into electricity. While still in the demonstration and early commercial stages, wave energy has considerable potential in regions with strong and consistent wave activity.

Tidal energy exploits the predictable movement of ocean tides, driven by gravitational interactions between the Earth, moon, and sun. Tidal range technologies, such as barrages and lagoons, use the rise and fall of water levels to drive turbines, while tidal stream generators harness the horizontal flow of tidal currents. Tidal energy offers a reliable and predictable renewable resource, particularly in locations with significant tidal ranges or fast-moving currents.

Ocean thermal energy conversion (OTEC) takes advantage of the temperature difference between warm surface waters and cold deep waters in tropical regions. OTEC systems use this gradient to produce electricity through heat exchange and vaporization processes. Although technically complex and limited to specific geographic areas, OTEC has the potential to provide baseload power and support desalination.

Salinity gradient energy, or blue energy, generates electricity from the difference in salt concentration between seawater and freshwater at river mouths or estuaries. Technologies such as pressure retarded osmosis and reverse electrodialysis are being explored to harness this resource.

Each type of ocean renewable energy presents unique technological, environmental, and regulatory challenges. Continued research, innovation, and supportive policy frameworks are essential for realizing the full potential of ocean energy as a sustainable pillar of the Blue Economy.

Policy Incentives for Marine Energy Innovation

Policy incentives are critical drivers for accelerating innovation, investment, and deployment of marine renewable energy technologies. As countries seek to diversify their energy mix and achieve climate targets, targeted policy measures help overcome market barriers, de-risk early-stage development, and stimulate private sector engagement in the marine energy sector.

One of the most widely used policy incentives is financial support for research, development, and demonstration. Public funding, grants, and subsidies enable universities, research institutes, and private companies to develop and test new technologies, conduct feasibility studies, and address technical challenges unique to marine environments. These programs often prioritize projects with the potential to reduce costs, enhance efficiency, and minimize environmental impacts.

Feed-in tariffs and power purchase agreements provide guaranteed prices for electricity generated from marine renewable energy sources over a fixed period. By offering revenue certainty, these incentives attract investment, lower the risk for project developers, and support the commercialization of innovative technologies such as offshore wind, wave, and tidal energy.

Investment tax credits and accelerated depreciation schemes reduce upfront capital costs, making marine energy projects more financially viable. These fiscal measures are especially important for capital-intensive sectors like offshore wind, where significant resources are required for infrastructure, installation, and grid connection.

Market-based mechanisms, such as renewable portfolio standards (RPS) and carbon pricing, create additional incentives for utilities and energy companies to invest in marine renewables. RPS mandates require a certain percentage of electricity to come from renewable sources, while carbon pricing internalizes the environmental costs of fossil fuel use, making renewables more competitive.

Supportive regulatory frameworks further facilitate marine energy innovation. Streamlined permitting processes, clear environmental standards, and coordinated spatial planning reduce administrative burdens and uncertainty for developers. Governments may also establish dedicated agencies or "one-stop shops" to guide projects through regulatory requirements.

Public-private partnerships and international collaboration are increasingly used to leverage expertise, share risks, and pool resources. Collaboration with local communities and stakeholders ensures that marine energy projects align with social, economic, and environmental priorities.

By combining financial incentives, supportive policies, and collaborative approaches, governments can accelerate the development and deployment of marine renewable energy, positioning it as a key pillar of the Blue Economy and contributing to a more sustainable and resilient energy future.

Regulatory and Environmental Considerations

The development of marine renewable energy—such as offshore wind, wave, and tidal power—requires robust regulatory and environmental frameworks to balance technological advancement, environmental protection, and the interests of multiple stakeholders. Clear, predictable regulations and rigorous environmental assessments are essential for ensuring that marine energy projects are safe, sustainable, and socially accepted.

At the core of regulatory considerations is the permitting process, which authorizes the construction and operation of marine energy installations. This process typically involves multiple government agencies and addresses a range of issues, including site selection, navigation safety, fisheries management, and alignment with marine spatial plans. Streamlined and transparent permitting can reduce administrative delays and investment risks while upholding safety and compliance standards.

Environmental impact assessments (EIAs) are mandatory for most marine energy projects. EIAs systematically evaluate potential effects on marine habitats, species, water quality, and ecosystem processes. They consider both the construction and operational phases, identifying potential risks such as habitat disruption, underwater noise, collision risks for marine mammals and birds, and the introduction of invasive species. Mitigation measures—such as seasonal restrictions, exclusion zones, and monitoring programs— are often required to minimize impacts.

Marine energy developments must also comply with international, regional, and national environmental laws and policies. Key instruments include the UNCLOS, the Convention on Biological Diversity (CBD), and relevant regional agreements. These frameworks provide guidance on the conservation of biodiversity, the prevention of pollution, and the sustainable use of marine resources.

Stakeholder consultation is a critical part of regulatory and environmental processes. Early and meaningful engagement with local communities, Indigenous Peoples, fishers, conservation groups, and other affected parties helps identify concerns, integrate traditional and local knowledge, and build support for projects. Transparent communication and participatory decision-making are vital for fostering trust and minimizing conflict.

Ongoing monitoring and adaptive management are required to assess the actual impacts of marine energy projects and ensure compliance with regulatory requirements. Feedback from monitoring informs future project design and regulatory adjustments, supporting continuous improvement.

Ongoing monitoring and adaptive management ensure that actual impacts of marine energy projects are assessed and that regulatory requirements are met. Feedback from monitoring informs future project design and regulatory adjustments, supporting continuous improvement. Robust oversight, strong environmental safeguards, and stakeholder involvement enable marine energy development to advance in a way that protects ocean health, supports innovation, and delivers sustainable benefits within the Blue Economy.

Integration with Coastal and Island Economies

Integrating marine renewable energy into coastal and island economies offers significant potential for sustainable development, energy security, and climate resilience. Coastal and island regions are often highly dependent on imported fossil fuels for electricity generation, resulting in high energy costs, supply vulnerabilities, and considerable greenhouse gas emissions. Harnessing local ocean energy resources—such as offshore wind, wave, and tidal power—provides a pathway toward greater self-sufficiency, lower emissions, and more resilient economies.

The adoption of marine renewable energy supports economic diversification by creating new industries, jobs, and value chains in coastal and island communities. Infrastructure development, such as the construction, maintenance, and operation of offshore energy installations, stimulates local business activity and enhances technical and engineering skills. Partnerships between project developers, governments, and local enterprises further strengthen the social and economic fabric of these regions.

Energy access and affordability are critical concerns in many island settings, where small-scale and decentralized energy systems are common. Marine renewable energy can supply reliable and cost-competitive electricity, reducing reliance on imported fuels and helping to stabilize or lower electricity prices over time. Microgrids and hybrid systems that combine marine renewables with solar, wind, or storage technologies are especially well-suited to remote or off-grid communities, increasing energy resilience and reducing vulnerability to external shocks.

The integration of marine energy also supports broader sustainability goals. By reducing dependence on fossil fuels, coastal and island economies can lower their carbon footprints and contribute to national and global climate targets. Renewable energy development can be aligned with environmental stewardship by prioritizing low-impact technologies, protecting sensitive habitats, and engaging communities in decision-making.

Capacity building and workforce development are vital components of successful integration. Training programs, technical education, and knowledge exchange initiatives enable local residents to participate in and benefit from new opportunities in the marine energy sector. Strengthening local expertise and institutional capacity supports the long-term viability and adaptability of these projects.

Collaboration with stakeholders—including government agencies, utilities, businesses, and community groups—ensures that marine renewable energy projects reflect local priorities, address potential conflicts, and maximize shared benefits. Effective integration positions coastal and island regions as leaders in the transition to a low-carbon economy while supporting inclusive and sustainable development within the Blue Economy.

Advances in Offshore Wind, Wave, and Tidal Energy

Rapid technological advances in offshore wind, wave, and tidal energy are transforming the potential of ocean-based renewables to contribute to clean energy systems and the Blue Economy. As demand for low-carbon solutions grows, these sectors are experiencing significant innovation in design, efficiency, and scalability, unlocking new opportunities for coastal and island regions.

Offshore wind has achieved the most widespread deployment and commercial maturity among marine renewables. Modern turbines have grown larger and more powerful, with rotor diameters exceeding 200 meters and individual units capable of generating more than 15 megawatts. Floating platform technology is extending the reach of offshore wind farms into deeper waters, where wind resources are stronger and more consistent. Advances in foundation design, installation techniques, and grid integration are driving down costs and improving project feasibility, making offshore wind a central pillar of energy transition strategies in Europe, Asia, and the Americas.

Wave energy is progressing from experimental prototypes to early-stage commercial projects. A variety of device types—such as oscillating water columns, point absorbers, and attenuators—are being tested and refined to withstand harsh marine environments and capture energy efficiently across different wave conditions. Improvements in materials, mooring systems, and maintenance approaches are enhancing reliability and reducing operational costs. As understanding of optimal siting and environmental impacts improves, wave energy's role is expected to grow in regions with high wave activity.

Tidal energy benefits from the predictability of tidal cycles, providing a stable and reliable source of power. Tidal stream generators, which operate like underwater wind turbines, and tidal range projects, such as barrages and lagoons, are both advancing technologically. Recent innovations focus on increasing efficiency, minimizing ecological impacts, and reducing installation and maintenance costs. Modular, scalable tidal devices are enabling deployment in a broader range of locations, including remote and off-grid communities.

Integration with digital technologies—such as remote monitoring, data analytics, and artificial intelligence—is optimizing performance, maintenance, and system management across all marine energy sectors. Coupling with energy storage solutions is improving grid stability and reliability.

The combined advances in offshore wind, wave, and tidal energy are accelerating the shift toward sustainable, ocean-based power generation, creating new jobs and economic opportunities, and supporting climate and energy goals worldwide.

Blue Carbon and Carbon Sequestration Initiatives

Blue carbon refers to the carbon captured and stored by marine and coastal ecosystems, particularly mangroves, seagrass meadows, salt marshes, and tidal wetlands. These habitats are among the planet's most effective natural carbon sinks, sequestering carbon at rates far higher than terrestrial forests and locking it away in plant biomass and sediments for centuries or even millennia. Recognizing and enhancing blue carbon storage is increasingly central to global climate mitigation strategies and the Blue Economy.

Mangroves, seagrasses, and salt marshes not only capture atmospheric carbon dioxide through photosynthesis but also stabilize and accumulate large amounts of organic matter in waterlogged soils. The anaerobic conditions in these environments slow the decomposition of organic material, allowing carbon to be stored for long periods. When these ecosystems are degraded or destroyed—through land conversion, coastal development, or pollution—the stored carbon is released back into the atmosphere, contributing to greenhouse gas emissions.

Blue carbon initiatives focus on protecting, restoring, and sustainably managing these critical habitats. Policy measures include establishing protected areas, regulating coastal development, and promoting ecosystem restoration projects that replant mangroves, restore seagrass beds, and rehabilitate salt marshes. These efforts not only enhance carbon sequestration but also deliver co-benefits such as biodiversity conservation, coastal protection, and support for fisheries and livelihoods.

Emerging carbon finance mechanisms are providing new incentives for blue carbon conservation. Projects that demonstrate measurable carbon sequestration can generate carbon credits, which may be sold in voluntary or compliance carbon markets. These credits create economic value for local communities, governments, and private investors, encouraging investment in conservation and sustainable management.

Research and monitoring are advancing the scientific understanding of blue carbon dynamics, supporting better quantification of carbon stocks and fluxes, and informing policy and market frameworks. International initiatives—such as the Blue Carbon Initiative and collaborations under the United Nations Framework Convention on Climate Change (UNFCCC)—are working to integrate blue carbon into national climate commitments and global carbon accounting systems.

Protecting and enhancing blue carbon ecosystems represents a powerful, nature-based solution for mitigating climate change, increasing resilience to sea-level rise and extreme weather, and supporting sustainable development within the Blue Economy.

Challenges and Opportunities in Scaling Marine Energy

Scaling marine renewable energy—such as offshore wind, wave, and tidal power—offers considerable opportunities for diversifying energy systems, reducing greenhouse gas emissions, and stimulating economic growth. However, expanding these technologies to commercial scale presents a distinct set of challenges that must be addressed for the sector to realize its full potential within the Blue Economy.

One of the main challenges is the high upfront cost of development, including research, infrastructure, installation, and grid integration. Early-stage marine energy projects often require significant investment and can face uncertainty around returns, especially in the absence of long-term policy support and stable revenue streams.

Securing financing and de-risking investments are essential for advancing large-scale deployment.

Technological challenges also persist. Harsh marine environments demand robust materials and innovative engineering solutions to ensure reliability, safety, and longevity of equipment. Issues such as biofouling, corrosion, and the need for efficient maintenance contribute to operational costs and technical complexity.

Regulatory and permitting hurdles can delay project development, particularly when environmental impacts and user conflicts need to be carefully managed. Achieving a balance between energy development, conservation, and other uses of marine space requires clear, coordinated regulatory processes and meaningful stakeholder engagement.

On the opportunity side, marine energy provides reliable, locally sourced power for coastal and island communities, reducing dependence on fossil fuel imports. Advances in technology and economies of scale are driving down costs, making marine renewables increasingly competitive with other energy sources. Integration with digital technologies, energy storage, and hybrid systems further enhances grid reliability and system flexibility.

Strong policy support, targeted research and development, and cross-sector collaboration are paving the way for marine energy to become a major contributor to sustainable energy transitions. Embracing these opportunities will help realize the environmental, economic, and social benefits of marine renewables within the Blue Economy.

Chapter 7: Maritime Transport, Ports, and Blue Economy Logistics

Chapter 7 examines the critical role of maritime transport, ports, and logistics in supporting the Blue Economy's growth and sustainability. As the primary mode for global trade, maritime transport connects markets, drives economic activity, and facilitates the movement of goods and resources worldwide. This chapter explores the environmental impacts of shipping and port operations, and the policy approaches and technological innovations aimed at greening maritime logistics. It discusses sustainable port development, decarbonization of shipping, and the integration of digitalization and smart shipping technologies to improve efficiency and reduce emissions. Additionally, the chapter addresses emerging trends in marine transport policy, highlighting the challenges and opportunities of building resilient, inclusive, and low-impact maritime supply chains. By focusing on the intersection of infrastructure, governance, and innovation, this chapter demonstrates how maritime transport and logistics are evolving to meet the environmental and economic goals of the Blue Economy.

The Role of Maritime Transport in the Global Economy

Maritime transport is the backbone of global trade and a vital enabler of economic growth, development, and integration. Over 80 percent of the world's goods by volume—including raw materials, energy resources, manufactured products, and food—are transported by sea, making maritime shipping the most cost-effective and energy-efficient mode for moving large quantities of cargo across vast distances.

The maritime transport sector consists of a complex network of shipping lines, ports, logistics providers, and supporting industries. Major trade routes connect continents, linking producers with consumers and resource-rich regions with manufacturing hubs. Bulk carriers, container ships, oil and gas tankers, and specialized vessels form the core of the world's merchant fleet, providing the infrastructure necessary for global supply chains to function smoothly.

Ports play a crucial role as gateways between sea and land, facilitating the transfer, storage, and distribution of goods. Efficient port operations, modern infrastructure, and advanced logistics systems are essential for minimizing delays, reducing costs, and supporting just-in-time delivery models. The competitiveness of national and regional economies is closely tied to the quality and connectivity of their port and maritime transport services.

Maritime transport supports not only international trade but also employment and economic activity. The sector provides millions of direct and indirect jobs in shipbuilding, port operations, logistics, insurance, finance, and regulatory services. Coastal and island nations in particular depend heavily on maritime transport for access to markets, resources, and essential supplies.

The sector faces growing demands for sustainability and resilience. Environmental concerns—including greenhouse gas emissions, marine pollution, invasive species, and the risk of accidents—are driving innovation in ship design, propulsion, fuel alternatives, and waste management. Decarbonization and digitalization are reshaping the future of shipping, with new regulations and technologies enabling more efficient and lower-impact operations.

Geopolitical and economic trends, such as shifts in global trade patterns, emerging markets, and supply chain disruptions, further influence the role and priorities of maritime transport. The COVID-19 pandemic highlighted both the vulnerabilities and adaptability of the sector, emphasizing the need for flexibility and contingency planning.

Maritime transport remains indispensable to the functioning of the global economy. Its ongoing evolution will be shaped by advances in technology, changing trade dynamics, and the pursuit of sustainability within the Blue Economy.

Sustainable Port Development and Operations

Sustainable port development and operations are fundamental to advancing the Blue Economy, reducing environmental impacts, and supporting resilient, efficient global trade networks. Ports serve as vital hubs for the transfer of goods, raw materials, and passengers, linking maritime and land-based transportation systems. As maritime trade grows and environmental challenges intensify, the sustainability of port infrastructure and activities has become a key priority for governments, businesses, and communities alike.

Modern sustainable ports integrate environmental stewardship, social responsibility, and economic performance into their design and daily operations. One of the core strategies is the reduction of emissions and pollution. Ports are increasingly adopting clean energy sources—such as onshore power supply for vessels, solar panels, and electrified cargo handling equipment—to lower greenhouse gas emissions, improve air quality, and comply with tightening environmental regulations. Shore-to-ship power systems allow ships to turn off their engines while docked, further reducing emissions and noise.

Waste management and water quality protection are also central concerns. Ports implement advanced systems to treat and recycle wastewater, manage stormwater runoff, and prevent spills of oil or hazardous substances. Many ports have developed protocols for handling ship-generated waste and ballast water, reducing the risk of marine pollution and the introduction of invasive species.

Biodiversity conservation is integrated into port planning through the protection and restoration of sensitive habitats, such as wetlands, mangroves, and coastal dunes. Environmental impact assessments and regular monitoring help minimize disruptions to local ecosystems and enable ports to adapt their practices as needed.

Sustainable operations extend to social and economic dimensions. Ports invest in workforce development, safety standards, and community engagement to ensure that local populations benefit from employment opportunities and infrastructure improvements. Public-private partnerships and transparent stakeholder dialogues foster innovation and the sharing of best practices.

Digitalization is transforming port operations, making them more efficient, transparent, and responsive to changing market demands. Smart port technologies—including automated cargo handling, real-time tracking, and integrated logistics platforms—improve operational efficiency, reduce congestion, and lower the carbon footprint of port activities.

Resilient port infrastructure is essential for adapting to climate change impacts such as sea-level rise, extreme weather, and changing shipping patterns. Ongoing investment in climate-proof design, flexible logistics, and emergency response planning supports continuity and competitiveness.

Sustainable port development is a cornerstone of a future-oriented Blue Economy, ensuring that ports continue to serve as engines of economic growth while safeguarding environmental and social well-being.

Decarbonization of Shipping

Decarbonization of shipping is a central objective in the transition to a more sustainable maritime sector and a critical element of the Blue Economy. As one of the world's largest transport sectors, shipping accounts for approximately 2–3 percent of global greenhouse gas emissions, primarily from the combustion of heavy fuel oil in ship engines. With the expected growth in maritime trade, reducing the carbon footprint of shipping has become a priority for industry stakeholders, regulators, and governments worldwide.

Regulatory frameworks are leading the decarbonization effort. The IMO has set ambitious targets for the sector, including reducing total annual greenhouse gas emissions by at least 50 percent by 2050 compared to 2008 levels, with an ultimate aim of phasing them out entirely. Mandatory measures—such as the Energy Efficiency Design Index for new ships, the Ship Energy Efficiency Management Plan, and the Carbon Intensity Indicator—set standards for vessel design, operation, and reporting to drive continuous improvement.

The development and deployment of alternative fuels are fundamental to decarbonization. Liquefied natural gas, biofuels, hydrogen, ammonia, and synthetic fuels are being explored and piloted as cleaner options to replace or supplement traditional marine fuels. Adoption of these fuels requires investments in supply chains, bunkering infrastructure, and onboard technologies, as well as careful assessment of lifecycle emissions and safety considerations.

Technological innovation is also playing a pivotal role. Advancements in hull design, air lubrication systems, wind-assisted propulsion, and energy-efficient engines can reduce fuel consumption and emissions. The integration of batteries and hybrid propulsion systems, as well as renewable energy sources such as solar panels and wind rotors, further support the shift toward low- and zero-emission shipping.

Digitalization and smart ship technologies contribute by enabling real-time optimization of routes, speeds, and fuel use, as well as predictive maintenance and emissions monitoring. These systems enhance operational efficiency and support compliance with regulatory requirements.

Collaborative initiatives—such as green shipping corridors, voluntary industry coalitions, and partnerships between ports, shipping companies, and technology providers—are helping to accelerate the transition. Financial incentives, research funding, and carbon pricing mechanisms further encourage investment in clean technologies.

The decarbonization of shipping is a complex, multi-decade undertaking requiring global cooperation, strong policy support, and sustained innovation. Achieving this goal will ensure that shipping remains an efficient, reliable driver of the global economy while contributing to climate change mitigation and a thriving Blue Economy.

Digitalization and Smart Shipping

Digitalization and smart shipping are revolutionizing the maritime industry, transforming how ships and ports operate, how cargo is managed, and how sustainability goals are achieved. The integration of digital technologies is making maritime transport more efficient, transparent, safe, and responsive, while supporting the sector's transition toward lower environmental impact and increased competitiveness within the Blue Economy.

At the heart of digitalization is the collection, processing, and sharing of real-time data. Advanced sensors, satellite communications, and the Internet of Things enable ships, cargo, and port equipment to be continuously monitored and connected. These technologies provide valuable insights into vessel location, engine performance, fuel consumption, cargo status, and environmental conditions, allowing for informed and timely decision-making.

Smart shipping systems use automation, artificial intelligence (AI), and machine learning to optimize ship operations. Automated voyage planning and route optimization algorithms calculate the most efficient paths, taking into account weather, sea conditions, and port schedules to minimize fuel consumption and emissions. Predictive maintenance powered by AI and big data analytics helps prevent equipment failures, reduce downtime, and lower repair costs.

Blockchain technology and digital documentation are streamlining logistics and supply chain management. Paperless bills of lading, cargo manifests, and customs processes reduce administrative burdens, speed up cargo handling, and minimize the risk of fraud or error. Enhanced traceability and transparency are particularly important for meeting sustainability standards and regulatory compliance.

Ports are embracing digitalization through smart port platforms, which integrate logistics, customs, traffic management, and terminal operations into unified digital systems. Automation of cargo handling, gate entry, and inventory management increases throughput, reduces congestion, and improves safety for workers and visitors.

Cybersecurity is an increasingly important aspect of digital shipping, as greater connectivity brings new vulnerabilities. Investing in robust security protocols, staff training, and risk management systems is essential for safeguarding digital infrastructure.

Collaboration across the maritime sector—including shipping companies, port authorities, technology providers, and regulatory agencies—is driving the development and adoption of digital standards and best practices. Pilot projects and digital innovation hubs are accelerating the deployment of next-generation solutions.

Digitalization and smart shipping enable the maritime industry to operate with greater agility, efficiency, and environmental responsibility. These advances are laying the groundwork for autonomous vessels, enhanced customer experiences, and a more resilient, sustainable global shipping network.

Environmental Impacts of Shipping and Ports

Shipping and port operations play a vital role in global trade, but they also exert considerable environmental pressures on marine and coastal ecosystems. As the volume of maritime transport grows, addressing these impacts is essential for the sustainability of the sector and the broader health of the ocean.

One of the primary environmental impacts of shipping is air pollution. Ships typically use heavy fuel oil, which emits sulfur oxides (SOx), nitrogen oxides (NOx), particulate matter, and greenhouse gases (GHGs) such as carbon dioxide. These emissions contribute to poor air quality in port cities, acid rain, and global climate change. Regulations by the IMO are tightening allowable emission levels, prompting the adoption of cleaner fuels, exhaust scrubbers, and alternative propulsion technologies.

Marine pollution from shipping includes oil spills, ballast water discharge, sewage, and garbage. Even small leaks of oil or hazardous cargo can have devastating effects on marine life and coastal habitats. Ballast water, used for ship stability, often contains invasive species that can disrupt local ecosystems when released in foreign ports. International agreements, such as the Ballast Water Management Convention and MARPOL, set standards for managing ship-borne pollutants and invasive species.

Noise pollution is another growing concern. Underwater noise from ship engines and propellers can disturb marine mammals, fish, and other sea life, affecting their communication, migration, and breeding behaviors. Ports themselves generate significant noise and light pollution, which can impact both wildlife and local communities.

Port infrastructure and expansion often result in habitat loss or alteration. The construction of docks, dredging of channels, and land reclamation can destroy wetlands, seagrass beds, and other sensitive habitats, reducing biodiversity and ecosystem services. Sediment disturbance and increased turbidity can further degrade water quality and harm aquatic organisms.

Waste management in ports is crucial to prevent pollution from solid and liquid wastes generated by ships and terminal activities. Many ports are investing in facilities and protocols for proper waste reception, treatment, and recycling to minimize environmental harm.

Efforts to mitigate environmental impacts include the adoption of green port initiatives, investment in renewable energy, electrification of port equipment, and ecosystem restoration projects. Environmental impact assessments, ongoing monitoring, and stakeholder engagement are vital to minimizing negative effects and promoting sustainable practices.

Reducing the environmental footprint of shipping and ports is a key step toward building a responsible and resilient maritime sector aligned with the principles of the Blue Economy.

Policy Approaches for Greening Maritime Logistics

Greening maritime logistics is a strategic priority for reducing the environmental footprint of global trade, improving supply chain resilience, and supporting the broader goals of the Blue Economy. Policy approaches to sustainable maritime logistics integrate regulatory, economic, and collaborative measures that address emissions, resource use, and environmental protection across shipping, ports, and related logistics services.

Regulatory frameworks set the foundation for greener logistics. International agreements—such as the IMO MARPOL Convention and its annexes—establish limits on air emissions, water pollution, and waste management for ships. New IMO regulations targeting SOx, NOx, GHGs, and energy efficiency standards are driving innovation in vessel design, alternative fuels, and emission control technologies. National and regional authorities complement these rules with additional requirements for port operations, cargo handling, and land-side transport connections.

Economic incentives encourage the adoption of green technologies and practices. Port authorities may offer discounts or priority berthing for ships that meet high environmental standards, such as those using low-emission fuels, shore-to-ship power, or advanced pollution control equipment. Emissions trading schemes, carbon pricing, and investment grants further incentivize efficiency improvements and the transition to renewable energy in port and shipping operations.

Integrated logistics planning aligns port development, shipping routes, and hinterland connections with environmental objectives. Investments in intermodal transport systems, digitalization, and automation enable seamless movement of goods, reduce congestion, and minimize emissions from idling and transshipment. Smart logistics platforms optimize cargo flows and enhance real-time visibility, supporting more efficient and sustainable supply chains.

Collaboration is key to successful greening initiatives. Stakeholder engagement—among shipping companies, port authorities, logistics providers, regulators, and local communities—ensures that policy measures reflect diverse interests, address operational challenges, and maximize co-benefits. Public-private partnerships and international knowledge-sharing accelerate the adoption of best practices and technological innovation.

Continuous monitoring, transparent reporting, and third-party certification strengthen accountability and drive improvement. Voluntary initiatives, such as green shipping corridors and eco-labeling for ports and logistics providers, help raise industry standards and increase consumer awareness.

Greening maritime logistics through effective policy approaches not only reduces environmental impacts but also enhances efficiency, competitiveness, and reputation across the shipping sector. These efforts are essential for building a sustainable, future-oriented logistics system within the Blue Economy.

Emerging Trends in Marine Transport Policy

Marine transport policy is evolving rapidly in response to technological innovation, shifting trade dynamics, and the urgent need for sustainability and resilience. Several emerging trends are shaping the future direction of the maritime sector, reflecting both global priorities and local challenges.

Decarbonization is a dominant trend, with policy frameworks increasingly focused on reducing greenhouse gas emissions from ships and ports. New regulations, investment in alternative fuels, and carbon pricing mechanisms are driving the adoption of cleaner technologies and more efficient operational practices. Initiatives such as green shipping corridors—dedicated routes for low- or zero-emission vessels—are being piloted to accelerate sector-wide transformation.

Digitalization is transforming marine transport policy, enabling real-time monitoring, predictive analytics, and integrated logistics management. The adoption of smart shipping technologies, blockchain for documentation, and digital port platforms is streamlining operations, enhancing transparency, and improving safety across the supply chain.

Resilience to climate change and disruptions is a growing focus. Policies are being developed to strengthen infrastructure, enhance emergency preparedness, and support flexible supply chains that can adapt to extreme weather, pandemics, and geopolitical risks. Ports are investing in climate-proofing and business continuity planning.

Social responsibility and inclusivity are increasingly embedded in marine transport policy. There is greater emphasis on workforce development, fair labor standards, gender equality, and engagement with local communities. These measures aim to ensure that the benefits of maritime growth are widely shared and that the sector attracts and retains talent.

International collaboration continues to be critical. Policymakers are working together through global forums and regional initiatives to harmonize standards, share best practices, and address transboundary issues such as marine pollution and invasive species.

Emerging trends in marine transport policy are positioning the sector for a future that is cleaner, smarter, more resilient, and socially responsible, supporting the sustainable growth of the Blue Economy.

Chapter 8: Pollution, Waste, and Ocean Health

Chapter 8 addresses the pressing issues of pollution, waste, and their profound impacts on ocean health, which are central challenges for achieving a sustainable Blue Economy. Marine pollution—from plastics and emerging contaminants to nutrient runoff and chemical discharges—threatens biodiversity, ecosystem services, and human livelihoods across coastal and ocean environments. This chapter explores the major sources of marine pollution, including land-based and ocean-based activities, and reviews the policy frameworks designed to control and reduce pollutant inputs. It highlights the importance of addressing land-sea interactions, marine litter, and plastics through integrated management and circular economy solutions. The chapter also examines emerging contaminants and the need for adaptive governance to tackle these new threats. Strategies for strengthening ocean health through pollution reduction, ecosystem restoration, and inclusive stakeholder engagement are discussed. By analyzing the complex relationship between pollution and marine ecosystem resilience, this chapter underscores the critical importance of comprehensive pollution control in securing the long-term sustainability and productivity of the Blue Economy.

Major Sources of Marine Pollution

Marine pollution originates from a variety of land-based and ocean-based activities, threatening the health of marine ecosystems and the services they provide. As human pressures on the ocean intensify, understanding the major sources of pollution is essential for developing effective strategies to protect and restore ocean health.

Land-based sources are responsible for the majority of marine pollution. Agricultural runoff carries nutrients, pesticides, and sediments into rivers and eventually the sea. Excessive nutrients—mainly nitrogen and phosphorus—cause eutrophication, leading to harmful algal blooms and oxygen-depleted "dead zones" that can devastate marine life. Urban wastewater and sewage discharges introduce pathogens, nutrients, and chemicals into coastal waters, posing risks to public health and aquatic organisms.

Plastic pollution is a high-profile and pervasive issue. Millions of tons of plastic debris—including bottles, bags, fishing gear, and microplastics—enter the ocean each year, accumulating on beaches, in surface waters, and on the seafloor. Plastics are ingested by marine animals, cause entanglement, and transport toxic substances through food webs, affecting species from plankton to whales.

Industrial discharges, including heavy metals, hydrocarbons, and persistent organic pollutants, enter the ocean through rivers, outfalls, and atmospheric deposition. Oil spills, whether from tanker accidents, drilling operations, or illegal discharges, have acute and long-lasting impacts on marine habitats, birds, and mammals. These pollutants can bioaccumulate in the tissues of marine organisms, posing risks to human consumers as well.

Ocean-based sources also contribute significantly to marine pollution. Shipping releases ballast water, bilge water, sewage, garbage, and hazardous cargo residues into the sea. The spread of invasive species via ballast water and hull fouling is a major ecological concern. Fishing activities can generate ghost gear—lost or abandoned nets and lines—that continues to trap and kill marine life for years.

Atmospheric deposition is another source, with pollutants such as mercury and nitrogen oxides traveling long distances before entering marine systems. Coastal development, dredging, and land reclamation disturb sediments and increase turbidity, further degrading water quality and habitats.

Emerging contaminants—such as pharmaceuticals, personal care products, and nanomaterials—are increasingly detected in the marine environment, raising concerns about their effects on ecosystem and human health.

Addressing the major sources of marine pollution requires integrated policies, technological solutions, international cooperation, and public awareness to safeguard the health and resilience of the ocean for future generations.

Policy Frameworks for Pollution Control

Effective policy frameworks for pollution control are essential for protecting marine ecosystems, human health, and the economic benefits that derive from a clean and productive ocean. These frameworks provide the legal and institutional basis for regulating, monitoring, and reducing the release of pollutants from both land-based and ocean-based sources.

International conventions form the backbone of global efforts to control marine pollution. The MARPOL, administered by the IMO, sets comprehensive standards for the discharge of oil, chemicals, sewage, garbage, and air pollutants from ships. The London Convention and Protocol further regulate the dumping of waste and other materials at sea, prohibiting or strictly controlling activities that could harm the marine environment.

Land-based pollution is addressed through agreements such as the Global Programme of Action for the Protection of the Marine Environment from Land-based Activities, coordinated by the United Nations Environment Programme (UNEP). Regional conventions— like the OSPAR Convention for the North-East Atlantic, the Helsinki Convention for the Baltic Sea, and the Cartagena Convention for the Wider Caribbean—facilitate cooperation among neighboring countries to tackle shared pollution challenges, harmonize standards, and coordinate enforcement and monitoring efforts.

National governments translate these international commitments into domestic law through environmental regulations, water quality standards, emission limits, and permitting systems for industries, agriculture, and wastewater management. ICZM and watershed-based approaches ensure that pollution control measures consider the connections between land, rivers, and the sea.

Economic instruments are increasingly used to complement regulatory measures. These include pollution taxes, fees, tradable permits, and subsidies for clean technologies, encouraging industries and communities to adopt practices that minimize pollution. Investments in green infrastructure—such as constructed wetlands, wastewater treatment plants, and stormwater management systems—help reduce the flow of contaminants into marine environments.

Monitoring, enforcement, and public participation are key pillars of successful policy frameworks. Transparent reporting, regular environmental assessments, and strong penalties for violations support compliance and accountability. Engaging stakeholders—including industry, local communities, and civil society—ensures that policies are practical, effective, and reflect local priorities.

As new threats such as plastic pollution and emerging contaminants arise, policy frameworks must remain adaptive and responsive. Continuous improvement, science-based decision-making, and international cooperation are vital for safeguarding ocean health and supporting the objectives of the Blue Economy.

Addressing Land-Sea Interactions

Land-sea interactions are fundamental drivers of marine ecosystem health and are a crucial focus for effective pollution control and integrated management. The activities and processes occurring on land—such as agriculture, urban development, industry, and forestry—directly influence the quality and quantity of water, nutrients, sediments, and pollutants that enter coastal and marine environments. Recognizing and addressing these connections is essential for sustaining ocean health, supporting biodiversity, and securing the benefits of the Blue Economy.

ICZM and watershed-based approaches are central to managing land-sea interactions. These frameworks promote the coordination of policies and actions across sectors and administrative boundaries, ensuring that land use planning, water management, and marine conservation are aligned. By viewing watersheds, river basins, estuaries, and coastal zones as interconnected systems, decision-makers can better anticipate and mitigate the downstream impacts of land-based activities on marine environments.

Pollution from agricultural runoff, urban wastewater, and industrial discharges is one of the most significant land-based threats to the ocean. Nutrient enrichment leads to algal blooms and hypoxic zones, while pesticides, heavy metals, and other contaminants threaten marine life and human health. Erosion and sedimentation from deforestation and construction can smother coral reefs, seagrass beds, and other sensitive habitats. Addressing these issues requires a suite of measures, including best management practices in agriculture (e.g., precision fertilization, buffer strips), green infrastructure in urban areas (e.g., rain gardens, permeable pavements), and effective wastewater treatment.

Restoration of natural landscapes, such as wetlands, mangroves, and riparian buffers, enhances the ability of coastal and upstream areas to filter pollutants, regulate water flows, and protect against flooding and erosion. Engaging local communities, landowners, and stakeholders in restoration and conservation efforts builds local ownership and strengthens the resilience of both land and sea.

Policy and regulatory instruments—such as zoning, land-use permits, and environmental impact assessments—should explicitly address land-sea connections and incentivize sustainable practices. Cross-sectoral governance, data sharing, and joint monitoring are essential for effective implementation.

Addressing land-sea interactions through integrated approaches reduces pollution, enhances ecosystem services, and builds the foundation for sustainable coastal and marine development. This holistic perspective is key to realizing the environmental and economic benefits of the Blue Economy.

Marine Litter and Plastics Policy

Marine litter, particularly plastics, has emerged as one of the most pervasive and visible forms of pollution affecting the world's oceans. Plastics make up a significant portion of marine debris, accumulating on shorelines, floating on the ocean surface, and settling on the seafloor. Their persistence, widespread distribution, and harmful effects on marine life and ecosystems have made plastics policy a global priority for ocean health and the Blue Economy.

Plastics enter the marine environment through a variety of pathways, including mismanaged waste, stormwater runoff, industrial discharges, and maritime activities. Once in the ocean, plastics break down into smaller fragments—microplastics—that are ingested by marine organisms, accumulate in food webs, and can impact fisheries, tourism, and human health. Lost or abandoned fishing gear, known as "ghost gear," continues to trap and kill marine life for years.

Addressing marine litter and plastics requires a comprehensive policy response at local, national, and international levels. Bans and restrictions on single-use plastics—such as bags, straws, cutlery, and microbeads—have been adopted by many countries to reduce the production and consumption of items that are most likely to become litter. Extended producer responsibility (EPR) schemes hold manufacturers accountable for the entire lifecycle of plastic products, incentivizing design for recyclability, collection, and proper disposal.

Waste management improvements are essential for reducing land-based sources of marine litter. Policies support investment in recycling infrastructure, waste collection systems, and public awareness campaigns to encourage responsible consumption and disposal. The promotion of circular economy principles—where materials are kept in use for as long as possible—can help reduce plastic waste and create new business opportunities.

International cooperation is vital for tackling marine litter that crosses borders. The United Nations Environment Programme (UNEP) leads global efforts through initiatives such as the Global Partnership on Marine Litter and the development of a binding international treaty on plastic pollution. Regional action plans, such as those developed under Regional Seas Conventions, foster collaboration among neighboring countries to monitor, prevent, and clean up marine litter.

Research and monitoring support effective policy by providing data on sources, distribution, and impacts of plastics in the marine environment. Stakeholder engagement—including industry, civil society, and local communities—ensures that policies are practical, inclusive, and widely supported.

Effective marine litter and plastics policy reduces pollution, safeguards marine biodiversity, and supports the health, productivity, and sustainability of the Blue Economy.

Emerging Contaminants and Ocean Health

Emerging contaminants—also known as contaminants of emerging concern—are a diverse group of chemicals and substances increasingly detected in the marine environment. Unlike traditional pollutants such as oil, nutrients, or heavy metals, emerging contaminants include pharmaceuticals, personal care products, hormones, microplastics, nanomaterials, flame retardants, pesticides, and industrial chemicals. Their presence in oceans is raising new questions about ecosystem and human health and presents complex challenges for policy and management within the Blue Economy.

These substances enter the marine environment through various pathways. Wastewater treatment plants often do not fully remove pharmaceuticals and personal care products, resulting in continuous, low-level discharges into rivers and coastal waters. Runoff from agriculture, urban areas, and industrial sites carries pesticides, herbicides, and other chemicals into the sea. Maritime activities contribute antifouling agents, cleaning products, and microplastics from shipboard operations. The persistence, bioaccumulation, and potential toxicity of many of these contaminants mean they can affect marine organisms—even at very low concentrations.

The impacts of emerging contaminants are still being understood, but evidence is growing that they can disrupt hormone systems, reproduction, and behavior in marine life, reduce immunity, and alter community structure. Microplastics and nanomaterials may act as carriers for other toxic substances and pathogens, magnifying their effects throughout the food web. There is also concern about potential risks to human health, particularly for communities that rely heavily on seafood.

Addressing emerging contaminants requires a precautionary and adaptive management approach. Improved wastewater treatment technologies, stricter controls on the use and disposal of hazardous substances, and the development of environmentally friendly alternatives are important policy measures. Encouraging responsible prescription, consumption, and disposal of pharmaceuticals and chemicals can reduce emissions at the source.

International collaboration on research, monitoring, and data sharing is crucial to identify priority contaminants, understand their fate and effects, and guide policy development. Standardized methods for detection and risk assessment will support better management and regulation.

Engagement with industry, healthcare providers, scientists, and the public is needed to raise awareness and promote best practices. Continued innovation and responsive policy frameworks will be essential for managing emerging contaminants and ensuring the long-term health of ocean ecosystems and the benefits they provide to people and the Blue Economy.

Circular Economy Solutions for Marine Environments

Circular economy solutions are transforming how marine environments are managed, moving away from the traditional linear model of "take, make, dispose" toward systems that prioritize resource efficiency, waste reduction, and sustainable use. The circular economy aims to keep materials and products in use for as long as possible, extract maximum value from resources, and minimize environmental impacts through recycling, reusing, and redesigning products and processes. Applying these principles in marine environments supports the Blue Economy, fosters innovation, and addresses pressing issues such as marine pollution and resource depletion.

A key strategy in the marine context is designing out waste and pollution from the outset. This involves rethinking product design, materials selection, and packaging to reduce single-use plastics, improve durability, and facilitate recycling or composting at end of life. For example, fishing gear and aquaculture equipment can be redesigned to minimize loss and improve traceability, reducing the problem of ghost gear and its impacts on marine life.

Promoting reuse and recycling is central to circular economy approaches. Ports and coastal communities are establishing collection systems for used nets, ropes, and other marine plastics, enabling them to be repurposed into new products such as textiles, construction materials, or even new fishing gear. Incentive programs, take-back schemes, and partnerships with industry can support the recovery and recycling of valuable materials.

The circular economy also emphasizes keeping biological resources in productive use. Initiatives such as the recovery of nutrients from fish processing waste or the cultivation of seaweed for bio-based products help close resource loops and reduce waste. Seaweed and shellfish farming, when integrated with other marine activities, can enhance ecosystem services, absorb excess nutrients, and provide sustainable raw materials for food, feed, or bioenergy.

Collaboration among governments, industry, researchers, and civil society is essential for scaling up circular solutions. Policy frameworks can support circular practices through extended producer responsibility, eco-design standards, green procurement, and investment in infrastructure for collection, sorting, and processing of marine materials.

Digital technologies and innovation platforms—such as blockchain for traceability, artificial intelligence for sorting, and online marketplaces for secondary materials—are enhancing transparency and efficiency across the value chain.

Embracing circular economy principles in marine environments drives resource efficiency, reduces pollution, and unlocks new economic opportunities, supporting a healthier ocean and a more sustainable future within the Blue Economy.

Strategies for Strengthening Ocean Health

Strengthening ocean health is essential for sustaining the ecological, economic, and social benefits that the ocean provides. Achieving this goal requires a multifaceted approach that addresses both immediate pressures and long-term resilience, integrating science, policy, technology, and stakeholder engagement.

One foundational strategy is the implementation of ecosystem-based management. This approach considers the cumulative impacts of human activities, maintains ecosystem services, and balances conservation with sustainable use. Marine protected areas, habitat restoration, and the conservation of biodiversity are key tools within this framework, helping to rebuild depleted stocks, safeguard vulnerable habitats, and support the resilience of marine systems.

Reducing pollution is another critical strategy. Policies targeting land-based and ocean-based sources—such as improved wastewater treatment, stormwater management, and bans on single-use plastics—help lower the influx of harmful substances. Promoting circular economy solutions further supports waste reduction and resource efficiency in coastal and marine environments.

Climate adaptation and mitigation measures are increasingly important for ocean health. Protecting and restoring blue carbon ecosystems, such as mangroves and seagrasses, contributes to both carbon sequestration and ecosystem resilience. Integrating climate risk assessments into marine planning and disaster preparedness ensures that ocean management remains robust in the face of change.

Stakeholder engagement and inclusive governance strengthen the legitimacy and effectiveness of ocean health strategies. Involving local communities, Indigenous Peoples, industry, and civil society in decision-making promotes shared stewardship and the integration of traditional knowledge.

Robust monitoring, data collection, and adaptive management underpin all efforts to strengthen ocean health. Timely scientific information guides responsive actions, supports transparency, and enables continuous improvement.

Collectively, these strategies work together to safeguard ocean health, secure the foundations of the Blue Economy, and ensure that marine ecosystems continue to provide benefits for current and future generations.

Chapter 9: Financing the Blue Economy and Future Marine Policy

Chapter 9 focuses on the crucial role of financing in enabling the growth and sustainability of the Blue Economy, alongside emerging directions for future marine policy. Sustainable ocean development requires substantial investment across sectors such as marine renewable energy, sustainable fisheries, coastal infrastructure, and ecosystem conservation. This chapter examines the diverse public and private financing mechanisms—including blue bonds, blended finance, impact investment, and insurance products—that mobilize capital while aligning financial returns with environmental and social outcomes. It highlights the importance of policy alignment and incentives to attract and de-risk investment, supporting innovation and equitable growth. Additionally, the chapter explores international collaboration and capacity building as essential components for expanding Blue Economy opportunities globally. Looking ahead, it outlines emerging policy trends focused on climate resilience, digitalization, inclusivity, and integrated governance. Together, these themes provide a comprehensive framework for understanding how strategic financing and forward-looking policy can unlock the full potential of the Blue Economy and ensure the ocean's health and productivity for generations to come.

Investment Needs for Blue Economy Growth

The expansion and sustainability of the Blue Economy depend on significant and strategic investments across a range of sectors—including sustainable fisheries, aquaculture, marine renewable energy, coastal infrastructure, ecosystem restoration, research, and innovation. Meeting these investment needs is crucial for unlocking the economic, social, and environmental benefits of ocean-based development while safeguarding marine ecosystems for future generations.

Infrastructure investment is a top priority. Modernizing and expanding ports, logistics hubs, and cold storage facilities increases efficiency, reduces waste, and supports the growth of sustainable maritime transport. Building resilient coastal infrastructure—such as flood barriers, green ports, and nature-based solutions—helps communities adapt to climate change and sea-level rise, while protecting valuable assets and livelihoods.

Investment in clean energy technologies—offshore wind, wave, tidal, and ocean thermal energy—drives the transition to a low-carbon economy. Early-stage funding, concessional finance, and public-private partnerships are needed to de-risk projects, support research and development, and accelerate commercialization. Dedicated finance for microgrids and decentralized energy systems is especially important for island and remote coastal communities seeking to harness local resources and improve energy access.

Sustainable fisheries and aquaculture require investment in science-based management, traceability systems, eco-certification, and value chain improvements. Financing for sustainable feed, selective breeding, and responsible aquaculture practices strengthens food security and supports livelihoods. Upgrading vessels, gear, and processing facilities further enhances efficiency and sustainability.

Restoring and conserving marine and coastal ecosystems—such as mangroves, coral reefs, and seagrass beds—depends on targeted investment in habitat restoration, monitoring, and community-based conservation programs. Blue carbon projects that generate tradable credits for carbon sequestration offer new sources of finance while delivering climate, biodiversity, and resilience benefits.

Research, innovation, and workforce development underpin long-term Blue Economy growth. Investment in ocean observation systems, digital technologies, marine biotechnology, and training programs builds knowledge, supports adaptive management, and fosters the next generation of ocean professionals.

Mobilizing investment at scale requires a mix of public, private, and blended finance. Innovative funding mechanisms—including blue bonds, impact investment, and concessional loans—can bridge gaps and leverage additional resources. International cooperation and capacity building ensure that developing countries and small island states can participate fully and benefit equitably from Blue Economy growth.

Strategic investment in sustainable ocean sectors delivers high returns in jobs, resilience, and natural capital, advancing prosperity and sustainability within the Blue Economy.

Public and Private Financing Mechanisms

Developing a robust Blue Economy depends on effective mobilization of both public and private financing to support sustainable ocean sectors, infrastructure, and conservation initiatives. A diverse array of financing mechanisms—ranging from traditional public funding to innovative market-based instruments—is needed to meet the investment demands of the Blue Economy while aligning financial flows with environmental and social goals.

Public financing, provided by governments and international organizations, remains essential for foundational investments in ocean science, research, data systems, regulatory capacity, and critical infrastructure. Grants, budget allocations, and concessional loans are used to support the establishment of marine protected areas, restoration of coastal habitats, fisheries management, and the development of climate-resilient infrastructure. Multilateral development banks, such as the World Bank and regional development institutions, play a key role in channeling funds and providing technical assistance for large-scale ocean projects, particularly in developing countries.

Private sector investment is increasingly important for scaling innovation, commercializing new technologies, and developing sustainable business models. Venture capital, private equity, and corporate finance drive the growth of marine renewable energy, aquaculture, biotechnology, and digital solutions for marine monitoring and management. Impact investors, who seek both financial returns and positive environmental or social impact, are helping to direct capital toward sustainable ocean activities, from eco-tourism to blue carbon projects.

Innovative financing mechanisms are bridging the gap between public and private funding. Blue bonds and green bonds raise capital for projects with defined sustainability outcomes, such as ecosystem restoration, pollution control, or clean energy. Payment for ecosystem services (PES) programs compensate communities or businesses for actions that protect or restore valuable marine resources. Insurance products, such as parametric insurance for coral reefs or fisheries, offer financial resilience against climate impacts and natural disasters.

Blended finance combines public and private capital to de-risk investments and attract additional funding, especially in emerging or higher-risk ocean sectors. Public guarantees, first-loss capital, and technical assistance grants can make projects more attractive to commercial investors and accelerate project development.

Enabling frameworks—such as transparent governance, clear regulations, and standardized sustainability metrics—are vital for building investor confidence and ensuring that financing supports genuine Blue Economy objectives. Collaboration among governments, financial institutions, industry, and civil society is crucial for scaling up resources and ensuring inclusive and equitable benefits.

Effective public and private financing mechanisms underpin the growth of sustainable ocean economies, supporting innovation, resilience, and long-term value creation for people and the planet.

Blue Bonds and Innovative Financial Instruments

Blue bonds and other innovative financial instruments are playing an increasingly important role in mobilizing capital for sustainable ocean projects and advancing the Blue Economy. These tools are designed to channel investment toward activities that benefit marine ecosystems, support climate resilience, and foster inclusive economic growth, while offering returns for investors.

Blue bonds are debt instruments issued by governments, development banks, or private entities specifically to finance ocean-related initiatives. The proceeds are earmarked for projects such as sustainable fisheries management, marine protected area expansion, coastal restoration, pollution control, and marine renewable energy. Blue bonds are modeled after green bonds, which have become a widely used vehicle for financing climate and environmental solutions on land. Transparent criteria, rigorous reporting, and independent verification are essential for ensuring that blue bond-funded projects deliver measurable environmental and social benefits.

Several pioneering examples have demonstrated the potential of blue bonds. The Republic of Seychelles launched the world's first sovereign blue bond in 2018, raising capital to support sustainable fisheries and marine conservation. The World Bank and other multilateral development banks have since issued blue bonds and structured innovative debt-for-nature swaps, where debt relief is exchanged for commitments to invest in ocean protection and sustainability.

Beyond blue bonds, a variety of innovative financial instruments are being developed. Impact investment funds target ocean solutions that generate both financial returns and positive outcomes for ecosystems and communities. Blended finance mechanisms combine public and private capital to de-risk investment in emerging sectors, such as marine biotechnology or sustainable aquaculture. Results-based financing, such as PES, links financial rewards to the achievement of predefined conservation or climate goals.

Insurance products tailored to marine risks—such as reef insurance or parametric insurance for fisheries—offer financial protection and incentivize investment in resilience-building measures. Digital platforms and tokenized assets are also emerging to facilitate investment, improve transparency, and expand access to blue economy projects.

Standardization of blue finance frameworks, robust governance, and transparent impact measurement are crucial to building investor trust and ensuring that financial flows contribute to genuine sustainability. Collaboration among governments, financial institutions, and the private sector supports the scaling and innovation of blue financial instruments.

Blue bonds and innovative finance mechanisms unlock new resources for ocean health, resilience, and sustainable development, driving progress toward a thriving and inclusive Blue Economy.

Mainstreaming Insurance and Risk Management

Insurance and risk management are increasingly recognized as vital components of the Blue Economy, supporting the resilience and sustainability of ocean-dependent sectors and coastal communities. As marine industries face escalating risks from climate change, extreme weather events, environmental degradation, and operational uncertainties, mainstreaming insurance solutions and proactive risk management is essential for safeguarding investments, livelihoods, and natural capital.

Marine and coastal areas are particularly vulnerable to hazards such as hurricanes, typhoons, sea-level rise, coastal erosion, and flooding. These risks threaten infrastructure, disrupt supply chains, and can lead to substantial economic losses. Traditional insurance products— covering vessels, cargo, and port facilities—remain important, but new insurance solutions tailored to emerging risks are expanding the toolkit for Blue Economy resilience.

Parametric insurance is one such innovation. Unlike traditional insurance, which compensates based on assessed losses, parametric insurance pays out automatically when predefined triggers—such as wind speed, wave height, or rainfall thresholds—are met. This allows for rapid response and recovery, minimizing the social and economic impacts of natural disasters. For example, reef insurance schemes provide immediate funding for restoration efforts following storm damage, helping maintain ecosystem services and community livelihoods.

Index-based insurance and catastrophe bonds are being used to protect fisheries, aquaculture, and coastal tourism against losses from adverse environmental conditions. These instruments can incentivize sustainable practices by linking coverage to the adoption of risk reduction measures or compliance with sustainability standards.

Risk management goes beyond financial products, encompassing strategies such as early warning systems, disaster preparedness planning, climate-resilient infrastructure design, and business continuity planning. Integrating risk assessment and management into policy, investment, and operational decisions strengthens adaptive capacity across marine sectors.

Collaboration among insurers, governments, industry, and communities is key to designing effective products, sharing data, and building local capacity for risk reduction. Public-private partnerships and technical assistance programs can increase access to insurance in developing countries and small island states, where coverage gaps are often greatest.

Mainstreaming insurance and risk management in the Blue Economy reduces financial vulnerability, supports rapid recovery from shocks, and encourages long-term investment in sustainable ocean development. These tools help build resilient marine economies, protect people and ecosystems, and secure the benefits of healthy oceans for present and future generations.

Policy Alignment and Incentives for Investment

Aligning policy frameworks and creating effective incentives are fundamental for unlocking the scale of investment required to grow a sustainable Blue Economy. Strategic policy alignment ensures that regulatory, fiscal, and planning measures reinforce each other, sending clear signals to investors, businesses, and communities about long-term priorities and opportunities in ocean sectors.

Coherent policy frameworks provide the enabling environment that de-risks sustainable investments and accelerates project development. This begins with clear, science-based regulations for resource use, environmental protection, and social safeguards. Transparent licensing, permitting, and spatial planning processes reduce uncertainty and administrative barriers for investors, while promoting responsible practices and stakeholder engagement.

Fiscal incentives are powerful tools for encouraging private sector participation and innovation. Tax credits, accelerated depreciation, investment grants, and concessional loans help lower the cost of capital for sustainable marine projects such as offshore wind farms, aquaculture facilities, eco-tourism ventures, and marine conservation initiatives. Subsidies can be targeted to support early-stage technology deployment, infrastructure development, and the adoption of best practices, provided they are designed to avoid market distortions or unsustainable outcomes.

Market-based incentives align financial returns with environmental and social objectives. Carbon pricing, tradable permits, and ecosystem service payments create revenue streams for projects that reduce emissions, restore habitats, or protect biodiversity. Public procurement policies that prioritize sustainably sourced seafood, renewable energy, or low-impact logistics send demand signals throughout supply chains and spur investment in sustainable solutions.

Cross-sectoral coordination enhances the impact of incentives and avoids conflicting policies. Collaboration among ministries of environment, energy, fisheries, transport, and finance helps integrate

Blue Economy objectives into national development strategies, infrastructure plans, and budget allocations. International alignment with global standards—such as the United Nations SDGs and the Paris Agreement—attracts development finance and signals long-term policy stability to global investors.

Enabling policies for financial innovation, such as frameworks for blue bonds, blended finance, or impact investment, expand the pool of available capital. Technical assistance and capacity building ensure that local entrepreneurs, communities, and small businesses can access incentives and participate fully in Blue Economy growth.

Well-designed policy alignment and incentives catalyze investment, drive sustainable innovation, and scale solutions that generate economic, social, and environmental benefits—laying the foundation for a thriving and resilient Blue Economy.

International Collaboration and Capacity Building

International collaboration and capacity building are foundational pillars for the sustainable growth of the Blue Economy, especially in a context where marine resources, challenges, and opportunities frequently cross national boundaries. Effective cooperation among countries, organizations, and stakeholders enhances the sharing of knowledge, technology, finance, and best practices, while capacity building empowers nations and communities to implement sustainable policies and innovations.

Oceans are inherently transboundary. Fish stocks migrate, ocean currents distribute pollutants and nutrients, and climate change affects ecosystems and societies across borders. International collaboration is necessary to address shared challenges—such as overfishing, marine pollution, biodiversity loss, and climate adaptation—through harmonized policies, coordinated enforcement, and joint research initiatives. Multilateral agreements, such as the UNCLOS, the Convention on Biological Diversity (CBD), and various regional seas conventions, provide the legal and policy frameworks for cooperation.

Joint action is also critical for effective marine spatial planning, fisheries management, search and rescue operations, and the conservation of areas beyond national jurisdiction. Collaborative scientific programs—such as international ocean observation networks and shared data platforms—improve understanding of marine systems and inform evidence-based decision-making. These efforts are increasingly supported by digital tools, remote sensing, and artificial intelligence, enhancing the capacity to monitor and manage ocean resources.

Capacity building ensures that all countries, especially developing nations and Small Island Developing States (SIDS), can participate fully in the Blue Economy and benefit equitably from its growth. This includes technical assistance, training, access to finance, and the transfer of technology for sectors such as aquaculture, marine renewable energy, pollution control, and ecosystem restoration. Building local expertise strengthens governance, enables innovation, and supports compliance with international standards and obligations.

Partnerships among governments, development agencies, research institutions, private sector actors, and civil society organizations are key to scaling up capacity building. South-South cooperation—sharing experiences and solutions among developing countries—has become an important avenue for peer learning and adaptation of best practices.

International collaboration and capacity building foster a sense of shared responsibility and stewardship for the ocean. These efforts accelerate progress toward global sustainability goals, support resilient and inclusive economies, and ensure that the benefits of the Blue Economy reach communities around the world.

Emerging Directions for Blue Economy Policy

Blue Economy policy is evolving rapidly to keep pace with dynamic environmental, technological, and socioeconomic changes. Several key directions are shaping the future of ocean governance and sustainable development, reflecting the need for greater integration, innovation, and inclusivity across all sectors.

Mainstreaming climate resilience is a central trend. Policymakers are embedding climate adaptation and mitigation into marine planning, fisheries, port operations, and coastal infrastructure. Protecting blue carbon ecosystems, advancing low-carbon shipping, and ensuring energy security through marine renewables are becoming core elements of national and regional Blue Economy strategies.

Nature-based solutions are gaining prominence, with increased investment in ecosystem restoration, marine protected areas, and circular economy initiatives that reduce waste and restore natural capital. Policies now emphasize the interconnectedness of land and sea, and the value of healthy ecosystems for economic and social well-being.

Digitalization and technological innovation continue to drive transformation. Policies are being updated to encourage the deployment of smart shipping, real-time data platforms, artificial intelligence, and ocean monitoring networks. These advances enhance decision-making, enable adaptive management, and open new frontiers for marine research and entrepreneurship.

Inclusive governance and equity are at the forefront of policy agendas. There is a strong push to ensure that benefits from the Blue Economy are distributed fairly, that Indigenous Peoples and local communities have a meaningful voice in decision-making, and that capacity building reaches the most vulnerable.

Integrated and cross-sectoral approaches are becoming standard practice, supported by international collaboration and alignment with the SDGs. Blue Economy policy is increasingly framed within holistic visions for climate resilience, biodiversity, economic prosperity, and social justice.

As the Blue Economy grows in scale and complexity, emerging policy directions will guide its evolution toward a more resilient, equitable, and sustainable ocean future.

Conclusion

The Blue Economy represents a transformative vision for the sustainable use, conservation, and equitable development of the world's oceans and marine resources. Throughout this book, the many dimensions of the Blue Economy have been explored, highlighting both the opportunities and challenges that arise as societies seek to balance economic growth, social inclusion, and environmental stewardship within ocean and coastal environments.

A key message is that the ocean's health and productivity are foundational to human well-being, food security, economic development, and climate resilience. Fisheries, aquaculture, marine transport, renewable energy, and coastal tourism all depend on healthy marine ecosystems and responsible governance. The rapid growth and diversification of ocean-based industries offer vast potential for job creation, poverty reduction, and innovation, particularly for coastal and island nations. However, these benefits can only be realized if development is pursued within ecological limits, ensuring that ocean resources are not depleted or degraded for short-term gain.

Strong and adaptive policy frameworks are essential for advancing the Blue Economy. International law, notably the UNCLOS, provides the legal foundation for marine governance, while a growing array of global, regional, and national policy instruments address issues ranging from fisheries management and pollution control to conservation, renewable energy, and equitable access. Effective governance requires clear rules, robust institutions, cross-sectoral coordination, and transparent stakeholder engagement. Mechanisms for monitoring, evaluation, and adaptive management enable continuous learning and improvement in the face of uncertainty and change.

Investment is another pillar of the Blue Economy's success. The scale of infrastructure, innovation, and conservation needed to support sustainable ocean development calls for significant financial resources from both public and private sources. Innovative financing mechanisms—such as blue bonds, blended finance, and impact investment—are expanding the pool of capital available for projects that deliver measurable environmental and social benefits. Aligning policy incentives, risk management tools, and enabling frameworks with sustainability objectives unlocks opportunities for business, investors, and communities to contribute to and benefit from the Blue Economy.

The path forward requires integrated, ecosystem-based, and participatory approaches. Protecting and restoring marine biodiversity, adopting circular economy solutions, reducing pollution, and building climate resilience are interconnected strategies that enhance both ocean health and economic prosperity. Inclusive governance that recognizes the rights, knowledge, and leadership of Indigenous Peoples, local communities, and small island developing states is vital for achieving fair and lasting outcomes.

International collaboration and capacity building underpin every aspect of Blue Economy advancement. The interconnectedness of marine challenges—climate change, pollution, resource management, and biodiversity loss—demands collective action and shared responsibility. Joint research, technology transfer, and knowledge exchange empower all nations to participate fully and equitably in the benefits of the Blue Economy.

As societies look to the future, the Blue Economy provides a powerful framework for realizing the promise of the ocean as a driver of sustainable development. With ambition, innovation, and cooperation, it is possible to build resilient marine economies that support people and planet, ensuring that ocean resources continue to sustain life, livelihoods, and opportunity for generations to come.